Free
to Be
Beautiful

Free
to Be
Beautiful

Ordinary Principles for an Extraordinary Life

KAREN B. FORD
& TINA KEIL

Publishing™

Dedication

To our daughters, Alison and Michelle

Acknowledgments

We'd like to especially thank:

Mike Keil and David Ford, who encourage us every day to live free to be beautiful. We love you.

Denise Hildreth, who took our words and made them sing. You are a kindred friend.

The leaders in the Classic Area, who were the reason for the "music" and who strive to live these principles as they lead and empower women.

And to the One who calls us daughters, Our Heavenly Father. We are honored to love You with our lives.

Table of Contents

Foreword

In a world focused on outward appearance and physical beauty, it's often difficult to remember that a truly beautiful life actually has very little to do with a number on the scale or what color to highlight your hair. In the hustle and bustle of everyday life, many of us have given away our power to dream the beautiful dream. We've allowed others to tell us who we are and who we ought to become.

In my life with John, I've had the opportunity to spend time with women all over the world. And in doing so, I've found that when all is said and done, we really all just want the same thing: the freedom to be real. A life filled with hope, dreams and purpose. But life isn't always easy. It's sometimes a little scary and sometimes a bit rough around the edges. But I can tell you this: A beautiful life is one that's worth fighting for.

In the following pages, Karen and Tina have captured the heartbeat of this message. Your life can be an exciting adventure if you allow yourself to dream the dreams that flow out of your purpose. You will find encouragement and renewed hope in *Free to Be Beautiful*. These ladies have provided you with a tremendous tool for finding your own inner beauty, no matter where you might be on life's journey.

So begin today. Turn the page and get ready to release the beautiful you.

- MARGARET MAXWELL

PART I

Discovering…

CHAPTER 1

When the Fairy Tale Crashes into Reality

*H*er mother had been in love with a wallpaper hanger. And the wallpaper hanger wasn't her father. Multiple nannies took Mommy's place most of the time.

When it was time to start school, she didn't fare much better there. In fact, at sixteen, she failed every standardized test. Nor did she make it in the world of ballet, which was her aspiration. She was too tall and lanky to become a ballerina.

So to make ends meet, she became a part-time kindergarten teacher, part-time housecleaner, and part-time nanny. Yet when she was only twenty years old, even though the odds seemed stacked against her, she married the man of her dreams, an ultimate prince charming.

He liked the sport of polo and had a nice smile. He seemed shy like her, yet opinionated. And he came from outlandish money. If it weren't for one "minor" character flaw, he would have been perfect: Prince Charming had a fondness for women—well, at least another woman besides her; a woman whom he continued to see even after he was married.

Discovering...

Even though their marriage produced two beautiful children, his affair produced a wife so desperate for attention and affection that she developed an eating disorder, had an affair or two of her own, and even tried to take her life.

Yet, in spite of all her pain, one fact remained that would never change: She was a princess. And no matter how her husband's actions made her feel, how her mother-in-law totally disregarded her, or how her own insecurities from an absent mother and dysfunctional family plagued her, no one could ever remove that title. She was the Princess of Wales. Or Princess Diana, as we called her.

Princess Diana lived her life serving her kingdom. In 1987, she opened London's very first medical unit for the sole purpose of administering care to AIDS patients. She took their hands and refused their shame. Some rebuked her. Others praised her. But those who were dying really didn't care that they were being loved by a princess; they were simply thankful to be loved at all.

Princess Diana tried to rid the world of land mines. She held children with missing limbs and relished their grateful smiles. She took flowers to the elderly and ladled stew for the children she met on her tour of Zimbabwe.[1]

Yet Princess Diana was never able to see her own true beauty. Although the world declared her to be one of its most beautiful people and although designers everywhere wanted her to wear their clothes, she could not see how beautiful she truly was. And though lepers and AIDS patients saw beyond her outward appearance to an inner beauty they rarely glimpsed, she never grasped it for herself.

Princess Diana's life was nothing like that of another woman, a woman she admired very much, the one with the wrinkled face and slumped shoulders. The one to whom children were drawn as if she were as beautiful as Princess Diana.

When the Fairy Tale Crashes into Reality

Mother Teresa's life ended shortly after Princess Diana's death. And while their hearts shared a similar passion for servanthood, their inner freedom was as different as their stature. Princess Diana lived in a self-made prison; Mother Teresa chose to live in a convent. Princess Diana graced the cover of many magazines; Mother Teresa graced the streets of squalor and the depths of society's filth. Princess Diana married the man of her dreams only to end up broken and abandoned—again; Mother Teresa surrendered her soul to the One of her dreams and found joy in ministering to the abandoned.

Mother Teresa understood the great perils of abandonment. She perceived it as an "awful poverty."[2]

Princess Diana drove sports cars and wore diamonds worth millions, yet lived with a destitute soul. Mother Teresa didn't own a car, and often wasn't even seen with a cross around her neck, yet she lived with her soul owning life's greatest possessions.

Both Princess Diana and Mother Teresa held the title of "princess." Both served their kingdoms well. Mother Teresa never graced the cover of *People* magazine's "Fifty Most Beautiful People" issue, yet she—more than Princess Diana—knew what it meant to live a life of joy and fulfillment, a life in which she was truly *free to be beautiful.*

Remember the first time you saw Snow White? She looked fabulous in that red lipstick. Remember the first time your mother read you the story of Cinderella? You would have killed for a fairy godmother like that.

Then when you were alone and no one was looking, you *were* a fairy tale princess. Did you steal away to your mother's closet and grab those gaudy, strappy heels before digging out your plastic tiara and baton to use for a magic wand? And in one beautiful afternoon, you were a princess.

Then you feigned sleep on your bed, or ran up the stairs in a vain attempt to beat the imaginary clock. And kissing you gently or running after you with exuberant gusto was your prince. And he was always perfect. Didn't always look the same, because that depended on which boy you were crazy about at the time, but he was always perfect.

And what woman wouldn't want to be like these fairy tale princesses? They were kind and honest and valued and well-known. And their men—well, who wouldn't want someone rich and noble and so indescribably handsome to chase evil away? Plus, those women wore some rather fabulous clothes and killer shoes!

And truth be told, for little girls, this was our filter for life: a fairy tale. Then came real life. And when life didn't measure up, many of us decided to forget about dreaming altogether. It's been said that by age twenty-two, most women have forgotten how to dream. Welcome to reality; it happens to the best of us.

Yet sometimes it's so much easier to see need in others than we could ever comprehend in ourselves. After all, we could see Princess Diana's need. What we once saw as the ultimate life of privilege, we began to look at with great pity. We pitied her pain. We pitied her depression. We pitied her bulimia. We pitied her marriage. And we would have had such wonderful advice for her—had she asked: "Girl, don't you see who you are? Why, you're a princess! Forget about that prince if he refuses to love you. He's not that great, anyway," we'd say. "Get on with life. Love will find you again. Enjoy your children. Enjoy your talents. You have such a good heart and such a kind soul. Just let that teach you how to dream again."

It would have been so easy to help Princess Diana set her course for victory, wouldn't it? Yet many of us, even now, have never realized that we are entangled in the same kind of unmet fairy tale that the Princess of Wales faced. We threw hope out the window years ago. And now, we've quit trying altogether.

When the Fairy Tale Crashes into Reality

We've trapped ourselves into a comparison game that convinces us we don't measure up. The beauty we once thought was possible is now nothing more than one of those fairy tales our mothers told us, and just about as unlikely as a fairy godmother who can turn mice into horsemen.

The unmet expectations are the only thing we expect anymore. And when we realize that it's impossible to cram our double-wide foot into that glass slipper, we begin to believe that there probably never was a slipper made for us anyway. We are certain we've been left out of the process completely.

So, instead of feeling like royalty, we feel like a royal catastrophe. And we begin to believe we have nothing to offer. We surrender ourselves to a life of *no*-effect. Better to stay home out of the game than to be the one who brings in the rainstorm. Well, that depends on our perspective.

Having a game called because of rain isn't always a bad thing. Sometimes rain can take a losing team and give it the time necessary to regroup, restrategize, reconnect, and remember.

When life starts to pour down on us, it's time to regroup our faith and remember what we believe in. It's time to restrategize so that we can avoid making the same mistakes once again. Reconnect with those people who help us find the value in ourselves. And remember— remember that we made it to the game because we were good.

Yes, we are here in this life—this game—because we've got something to offer. We got here because of a dream. That dream may be tucked so far back, we've forgotten all about it. Or maybe we've been afraid to surrender ourselves to the dream, knowing that it's going to require risk and sacrifice. It's time to change all that. Let the rain fall. It just gives us time to dig out those dreams and decide what to do with them.

Now, it is time to meet the challenge. You see, if a princess falls asleep because of a wicked witch's spell, only to wake up staring into the face of an enchanting prince, it isn't the worst thing that can happen, now is it? Neither is having a life of absolute surrender. You may have to make earthly sacrifices, but they will be saturated with eternal results and only heaven will reveal all your treasures.

Just like Princess Diana and Mother Teresa, we all want to live a beautiful life. But beauty isn't about good genes. Beauty isn't about a great heritage. Beauty isn't even about marrying a prince. Beauty is about the heart. Beauty is being willing to do what it takes and being brave enough to dream again. Beauty is about knowing where dreams come from and who really gives them.

But be warned as you take this journey. Just because you have a dream, your circumstances won't necessarily change. But because you have a dream, you *can* change your response to those circumstances. Now don't kid yourself. You're going to wake up tomorrow, and your breath will stink, the world will be better off if you put on some makeup, and no matter how hard you suck it in, the mirror may still reflect the Pillsbury Doughboy rather than a Victoria's Secret model. Life is still going to be life. But through these next few pages, our goal is to help you remember that you once had some desires of your own. And to remind you that being *free to be beautiful* is about what goes on inside of you.

∽

Like Princess Diana, the one thing that the pain of this world can never take away is your title. You are a princess. Whether the mirror reflects it or not, you are a beautiful princess. It just might be time to change mirrors. Take a look into the mirror of Truth, and you'll learn that God, the very one who fashioned you and formed you, is the King; therefore, you *are* a princess. There really is no other destiny you could have.

When the Fairy Tale Crashes into Reality

With such a title comes entitlement. Not entitlement to dictate or belittle. Not entitlement to wallow or hide. Not entitlement to be served. No, this is an entitlement of another kind. As a daughter of the King, you have been given an entitlement to dream and to love. An entitlement to choose and to grow. An entitlement to serve.

But when life paints your portrait for the world to reflect on, or just for your family to remember, our desire is that your painting will be even more beautiful than it is today.

"You know, the one thing I can say about that lady is that she may not have graced the cover of Vogue, but her picture looked fabulous underneath the magnet on the refrigerator. She never won the Nobel Peace Prize, but she won multiple hearts in our neighborhood. She didn't marry Prince Charming, but she never let him know it. And the lady at Neiman Marcus couldn't remember her name, but the lady at the grocery store checkout line lit up like a Christmas tree when she came through the door. And even though she was never Miss Universe, she was just as beautiful to me. In fact, she was *free to be beautiful.* It took her a while to believe it. But once she did, she never forgot it."

CHAPTER 2

I Want to Hear You Sing

TINA'S STORY

*M*ost of us have something that makes us feel valued. It's a gift or talent that sets us apart, makes us feel special. It's the glass slipper left on the fabulous stairwell. It's the smile that melts a thousand hearts. It's the ability to capture nature's beauty in oil or watercolor. It's the killer chocolate-chip cookie recipe that has earned you "Hangout House" of the neighborhood.

I had that something. It was the ability to sing. My parents loved me. I was certain of that. But I wanted to feel special, beautiful, known. I wanted to make a difference in life. And I believed the only way I could do that was with my voice. I never thought I was that good, but when I sang, I got attention, and that attention made me feel special. So, in my young perspective, I felt that singing was the *only* instrument that could bring about all those things I had ever dreamed and longed to become. I believed that singing would be my door to the castle, leading me to places people only dream of. And the older I grew, the more tightly I held to the value that it seemingly lavished upon me.

Discovering...

In those infamous teenage years, I grew in all the right places. I became curvy and began to attract the attention of the opposite sex. It was an ah-hah moment for me. I thought I had it all figured out: If you're thin and have boobs, people pay attention. I liked it. The attention made me feel noticed. Not special, but noticed. So, I began to realize that my previous perspective had been incomplete. I decided that with my singing and the right man, I would feel valued.

When I hit fifteen, I fell madly in love with Michael Edward Keil. He was an *older* man. He was twenty-one, and I was hopelessly in love. He was my dream man: handsome, ambitious, and a drummer. And in July 1980, six days after my eighteenth birthday and only one month after my high school graduation, my "drummer boy" and I drove off into the sunset.

But the white stallion that was supposed to carry me to palatial palaces and ballroom dances brought me instead to a life of cleaning house, cooking meals, working real jobs, and dealing with buried insecurities. It only took three short months of wedded bliss for those insecurities to present themselves again. In those early years of our marriage, Mike was a workaholic. My old fears of having nothing of value to offer permeated me with the worry that Mike would leave me. So I set a determined course of action. I decided I would be the best wife, best cook, best housekeeper, best lover this man could ever know. I scheduled my life around Mike's. I wanted to be completely available to him.

I had no idea that too much of a good thing can cause someone to become nauseated and avoid it all together. My every attempt to please seemed to cause Mike to retreat. This only increased my insecurities, which made me try even harder. It was a never-ending cycle.

I had made myself so convenient, he only desired me when it was, well, convenient. How convenient! How miserable! The more I lived for his approval, the more we grew apart.

Every day, I was bombarded with the same old questions in my mind: *Will I ever be special? Will I ever have enough value to measure up?* Every day I reminded myself how ordinary, how average I was. And I just knew that average wasn't good enough on anybody's scale.

For nineteen years, we played this song and dance. And then in 1999, the orchestra grew bored and left the building. And there we were facing each other. And it wasn't pretty. Everything in our life felt as if it was falling apart. And the repercussions of it all were ravaging our lives, our home, and our business.

Time doesn't permit me to tell you what that hell looked like, but nothing about it was beautiful. And the thought of being alone scared me to death. The reality that we now faced seemed to mean certain destruction for all involved. At that point, I think we may have even wanted the destruction if it meant ending the pain we were in.

But, believe it or not, in the middle of the desperation I still had an ounce of hope. And that was what I clung to. Even in the middle of a life that appeared to lack true worth, there was still something inside of me that knew a large part of this had to do with me. I knew I had to change my way of thinking and set a different course of action for myself.

Having been a Christian for years and having allowed that relationship to grow over the course of my life, I had a level of commitment that I knew was no longer optional. As with anything that you desire, in order to receive the maximum return, you must be willing to invest the best of yourself as well. So, that is what I did. I began to set aside each morning to read and talk with God. Each day I asked Him to give me more than an ounce of hope.

At this point in our marriage, Mike and I began counseling. After five months, our counselor finally confronted me with what he felt was one of my core issues. "Tina, I don't know how you are going to take this," he said, treading lightly but clearly. "But, you are an idolater.

You are living for a man and longing to be worshipped by someone who cannot make you whole."

Had it not been so true I might have slapped him. But instead, tears just rolled down my face. I could barely breathe. The word "idolater" wouldn't make its way to my lips for more than two weeks. And that was only said when I was alone and only I could hear it. It would be months before I could share what I had begun to realize as the truth. And as hard and harsh as it sounded coming from our counselor that day, the truth is those words were used to free me, free to be beautiful.

❧

And they all lived happily ever after. Not on your life! Things just got real from that point on. And sometimes the journey to "real" is just as difficult as the discovery that becoming real is even necessary. I realized that not only had I placed Mike in a position he was unable to attain, I had also given music its own position of dominance in my life.

Remember, I always believed people liked me when I sang. Just like I believed Mike would love me if I performed all my "duties" with grace and gusto. So, as much as I had to release Mike, I also had to let go of my music.

Even after a year of counseling, life seemed nothing but more miserable. And even though it had been a full year since I had laid music aside with the belief that I would never sing again, I still felt fearful and worthless. Then the phone rang.

"Tina, I can't get you off of my mind." Pastor Ray's voice came from the other end. "Will you sing during the offering tonight?"

Before I knew what I was saying, I told the pastor that I would sing. But what I didn't tell him—or anyone else for that matter—was that just that day I had decided it was time to end my marriage. I had had it. I was angry and felt I had every right to feel that way. I was hurt and sick and tired of hurting. It was over. I had no biblical reason for divorce, but on that day, I didn't want a reason. I was *mad!* God and I had been fighting this one out all day long before Pastor Ray called.

Lord, I've had it! I told Him. *I can't do this any longer; don't make me change my mind. Leave me alone about this. I'm through!*

So, as I drove to church that night, I was convinced I was in a bunch of trouble. I had argued with God all day, and I was certain that as soon as I got three or four steps up to the platform, I would either fall down the steps, forget all the words, or worse, be struck dead in front of all those people. You laugh, but I had seen it before. Two years earlier, I had been a guest soloist in a church and the choir was singing before me. Another soloist in the choir was singing, "I want to see Jesus . . ." and about that time, he fell down dead. True story. So I was certain it could happen to me. I did realize that it was this man's appointed day to go to be with God, but I sure had it on my mind as I drove to church that night.

When we reached the church, one of the pastors was there to pray with us. With no idea what I had just declared to God that day, he looked at me and said, "How are you, Tina?"

I looked at him in my shame and said, "Pastor Tim, I am so not worthy of being on that platform tonight."

Now I was certain I had just given him reason to tell me, "Be gone thou wicked woman who is not worthy of this platform!" But he failed.

He simply said, "Tina, none of us are worthy to be on that platform."

He was right. So I sang. I didn't forget any words. I didn't fall down the stairs. And I didn't die after the second chorus.

The next day, I sat across from my counselor and relayed to him the events of the night before. He said, "Tina, do you know what I think happened?"

"What?" I asked.

"I think God looked at you yesterday and said, 'Look at my girl. Listen to what she's saying. She's completely forgotten who she is, and she's forgotten she's my girl. I think I want to hear her sing.' "

Nothing prepared me for that moment. Nothing prepared me for the gift those words would give me. They took me to my value. They took me to my worth.

Eventually, those words also led to the restoration of my marriage. And they continue to lead Mike and me even today through the effort of growing and building the marriage that we were created to have.

You see, the beautiful thing about Prince Charming is that when Cinderella ran away from him, he didn't say, "Okay, nice girl, nice evening, who's next?" No, Prince Charming went after Cinderella. Even though she thought that once the glitzy gown was nothing but a well-worn slip dress and the tiara was nothing more than locks of mousy brown hair and the horsemen were really a bunch of rats, the prince wouldn't see anything in her worth keeping. But he did. How do we know? Because when he arrived at her home she was just Cinderella—no fancy trappings or magical fairy dust. And he stayed. Not only that, he didn't just stay, he asked if she would hang out with him forever.

And you know what I think? I think that if Cinderella had never lost that slipper, the prince would still have pursued her. Even if you never have your name on the front of a CD cover, if you never win an award for your great intellect, if the only people to know you exist are the ones you gave birth to, Someone still searches for you simply because He's crazy about you. Not your dress. Not your money. Not your style. Not your talents. *Just you.* Crazy about you. That kind of love frees you to love the same way. And who loves you in such a way? Only One, the One who created you. The One who calls you daughter. The one who is King to a princess.

Looking back, I can see that in those early years of my marriage, my motives were rarely pure. I didn't love Mike unconditionally. Oh, you would have thought I did. You would have said, "Look at Tina. Isn't she the perfect wife and devoted mother?" But right actions with wrong motives are nothing more than a pile of mess. Because in reality, when Mike didn't respond the way I wanted him to in order to fill my need of affirmation, I became even more demanding and determined to get what I wanted the way I wanted it.

Aren't we something? Many of us are too afraid for others to see the authentic us. We paint ourselves up with fancy clothes and nice cars and well-adorned conversations; we want the world to see us in a certain way: perfect and desirable. But when the clock strikes midnight and we know it's time to expose our flaws, we run in terror, even from the One who created us. And even though everyone else would let us run, God pursues. Why? Who can explain such love?

He wanted me. Not Tina the singer. Not Tina the extraordinary wife. Not Tina the fabulous mother. No, He wanted Tina the insecure. Tina the one in desperate need. Tina the girl who just wanted to feel like a princess. And He showed me that I *was* a princess. I was *His* princess. And He couldn't get me off of His mind. So, much so that He said, "I just want to hear her sing."

CHAPTER 3

Can I Call You Sometime?

KAREN'S STORY

"*I*'m going to start a new business!" I declared to my husband, David.

He looked at me as if I had two heads. After all, I was the same woman who had had the same hairstyle for the last ten years, had taught at the same school in the same classroom with the same bulletin board, all while my desk remained in the same exact place. I didn't drive myself anywhere except to work and back. And I only did that in the daylight. Nighttime never caught a glimpse of me behind the wheel. I was not what you would call an independent, outgoing person. The words "risk" or "change" weren't even in my vocabulary. But I, "Miss Monotony", was about to make a change.

It had started innocently enough in a department store. Shouldn't everything? The woman who had started a conversation with me was elegant, poised, confident, and outgoing—*everything* that I wasn't at that time. After a few minutes, she told me that she was a beauty consultant. When I heard that, I wondered how quickly I could make it to the exit. I was a woman who only wore makeup on special occasions. As I was frantically looking for the closest escape route, my beautiful new friend asked if she could call me. "Sure," I blurted. She offered her card in exchange for my number. And I was certain I would never hear from her again.

I was wrong. Virtually every week for the next six months this woman would call just to see how I was doing. I was always polite but always distant. Each time she called, she would invite me to go with her to one of her consulting events. She thought I would be a great fit in her cosmetic business. I always came up with fabulously creative excuses. Once I had to help the neighbor find her cat that had gotten lost (which he honestly had). Another time I had actually committed to go with her but called it off on account of rain. Granted it was only a tiny black cloud that had passed over the sun, but it looked like rain enough for me. Each excuse offered me a momentary reprieve. And I grew confident that I did not want anything to do with her business.

But then life happened in a big way. And when it did, I wasn't prepared. Up to this point, I had been very comfortable with my life. It wasn't exciting, but it was mine.

But then my son Justin was born and was diagnosed with a heart problem. I needed to take an immediate leave of absence from my teaching job and, like most families who live paycheck-to-paycheck, we had to start looking for other options. After only a few weeks, we were borrowing from Visa to pay MasterCard. And there I was, worried about my son, stressed about my finances, longing to give my daughter the future I wanted her to have, and none too happy about my world turning upside down in a matter of weeks. I missed the feeling of contributing to my family's finances. Truth be known, I even missed the mundane routines of my teaching job.

And right in the middle of all this, my friend from the department store called. I hadn't heard from her in a couple of weeks. And on this day, she caught me in rare form. I was sleep deprived, tired of Bert and Ernie, desperate for a miraculous check to find its way to my mailbox, and longing for some adult conversation. Yet, my friend knew nothing of how our lives had recently changed.

She told me that I had been on her mind lately, and then she said, "Karen, I'm going to be in your area next Tuesday. Would it be okay if I stopped by to see the baby and spend a few moments with you?"

"That would be fine," I said. And this time I meant it.

When she realized that I had agreed to see her, I think she was surprised. My word, I had tormented the woman for months! She paused for a moment, but she quickly recovered. And the next Tuesday, true to her word, she rang my doorbell.

That afternoon I was primed to hear what she had to say. She shared with me how her business worked, and, shocking myself, I thought, *Maybe this could be an answer for me.* It would allow me to set my own hours, giving me the flexibility to be home with my baby boy, and make an immediate fifty dollars a week.

Before she left, I wrote her a check and hoped it wouldn't bounce from here to the east coast. But for some reason, I felt that maybe I *could* do what she had talked to me about. Even if I just made fifty dollars a week, I thought it could at least help my family until I could go back to my *real job* as a schoolteacher.

How could I do this and not talk to anyone first? My thoughts began to race. How can I do this and not have to drive myself anywhere? How can I do this and not even wear cosmetics myself?

"I know I can't do this!" I called out in a vain protest to her as she headed to her car. "I know I'll be allergic to this product." I was certain I was breaking out in hives already.

"No, you're not," she consoled me. "I'll show you how you can use it." She drove away with a smile.

Discovering...

And later that night, I stood in the kitchen and told my husband
I had started a new business selling cosmetics. He examined the
material she had left with me and said he felt it would be worth
a try. This was as much out of character for David as my agreeing
to do it. After all, he knew me. He knew me well.

He knew that I wasn't the risk-taker type. He also knew that
I didn't have the money for the investment that I would need to get
started. So the plan was simple. I would start my new business with
the intention of quitting. Now how is that for a plan? I decided that
I would work for one year, telling as few people as possible about the
product. Then, when it came time to re-sign my teaching contract,
all would be forgotten.

A year passed and the contract time arrived. But something else
had arrived by that time, too: an enjoyment in life. During the past
year, I had worked *very* part time and made significantly more
money than I had made as a teacher. And more importantly, I had
a real sense that I was making a difference in the lives of those
I was privileged to work with. Life seemed to have a purpose. So,
taking a step of faith, I gave up my teaching position and turned
all of my energies to my new business. There was a certain amount
of fear, but an even greater sense of peace.

The next few years were filled with success! My business grew
and I experienced the wonderful feeling of personal accomplishment
as it reached new heights and moved to new levels. And my personal
growth was just as rewarding. I was feeling confident and empowered
to set *big* goals, and then I was motivated to set even bigger goals as
I met each one. Life was wonderful!

Then it happened. I failed, and I failed publicly. I missed a *big* goal
in a very public way. I was devastated, humiliated, and completely
embarrassed. The goal had involved my whole team, and they had
worked with their heart and soul to help us meet that goal. My failure

bottomed out their belief in the dream, in themselves, and in me. Many quit, some just withdrew, and I watched everything I had worked so hard to achieve fall completely apart.

Any failure like that leaves you doubting everything. I doubted my decision to get into the business in the first place. I doubted my purpose. And I doubted that this was truly God's plan for my life. What had seemed so clear just months earlier was now clouded with confusion. I found myself stranded in a chair day after day, doing nothing. I didn't communicate with my team, and I didn't communicate with God. My dreams had been shattered, and I felt alone.

During that time, my husband had given me a gift to celebrate the victory. But I wasn't celebrating anything, so I simply put the gift in a closet and forgot about it. Yet, one day as I was wandering around my office with nothing constructive to do, I opened the closet and looked down at that gift on my shelf. When I opened it, I found a box, embossed with the words, *One Hundred Lessons on Leadership,* by John C. Maxwell.

I opened the box to find one hundred tapes and outlines for the tapes. My heart told me I was a leader. But my head pointed to my failure and said I was anything but a leader. I perused the titles and found one that interested me. I put it in and completed the entire lesson. When I was finished, I thought maybe I'd try another one. With that I was hooked. Over the next six months, I listened to every tape and completed every outline. What I learned gave me the renewed desire and confidence to get back in the game.

I started by communicating with one person from our team. I encouraged her to work toward her own goals and helped her to set up a plan to meet those goals. I began to look forward to talking with her. Each day I continued to listen to those tapes and complete the outlines.

Then, out of the blue, I was offered a new job. *Well,* I thought, *what could be more perfect?* This was the answer to my problems! I could just resign the old one, start over at the new one, and never again have to walk back into the arena where I had failed. I could save any ounce of pride I had left and move on to bigger and better things. So that evening I sat down to write my resignation letter. And each time I began, I never got past, "To whom it may concern." Every time I tried, the faces of the people I had brought to the business and made a part of our team popped into my mind.

I'd write a few words, throw it away, and then start all over again. Four hours later, I was still at "To whom it may concern." It was late, and I was tired. But I knew I needed to pray. It had been quite some time since I had really prayed. Oh, I had gone through the motions. But I was certain God wasn't listening and that no prayer was getting through. Yet the intensity of that moment made it clear I *needed* to talk with God. I got down on my knees and begged Him to help me find the words to resign. But He had another plan. He usually does.

He caused me to look back at the events of my day and in looking at that day, all I could see were its blessings. The whole thing had me annoyed. Those thoughts of blessing were getting in the way of what He and I needed to accomplish. Still, all I could see were the blessings. As I got up to leave the room, I wrote down three blessings that I felt had actually occurred during that day and then went to bed.

When I awoke the next morning, I was amazed that for the first time in months, my focus was on *possibilities* rather than my *problems.* I went back to pray that morning and actually had a real quiet time. It was there that I made a decision, a decision to write a letter of regret instead of resignation. I wouldn't be taking the new job. No, I would be rebuilding what one moment of failure had attempted to destroy.

From that point on, every day was a new step toward additional clarity. I began to apply some of what I had learned from Dr. Maxwell's tapes. Good things followed. I began to look forward to work and had a sense of accomplishment again that once had seemed to be forever gone. Looking back, I realized that I had not been abandoned and alone. God was there, even though I refused to acknowledge Him. During that time, He had carried me and gently and lovingly nudged me in the direction He intended me to go.

I did have to go back into that arena again. It was one of the hardest things I ever had to do. But God and I went together. And I built differently this time. I built with a different style and focus, realizing that God hadn't changed His mind or His purpose for me. I had been the one to change. The next year my unit doubled our retail production and became the first Million Dollar Unit in the state of Tennessee. The next year, we completed our second million-dollar year and went on to reach the goal of becoming what is known as a "National area." This was the "big goal" that we didn't reach before, the one that had caused me such pain.

As with any career, I've had my fair share of ups and downs and highs and lows. There have been times that I have questioned myself and wondered if this had truly been God's plan for my life. There have even been times when I simply wanted to quit! But each time I doubt, I remember that every time I show up for my part, He has shown up for His.

Through the years, I have seen a thousand faces of women much like my own. Women who have settled into life yet forgotten how to live. Perhaps you're one of them. Have carpools become the most exciting moment of your day? If you have children, you know the drill: wake-up calls, second wake-up calls, breakfast (whatever is in the front of the pantry), carpool, work, carpool again, dinner (whatever is closest in the freezer), bedtime baths, bedtime stories, bedtime, husband's needs, and somewhere in the midnight hour, if I'm not too tired, me.

But like every woman, you have been given a gift. Perhaps the years have buried your gift so deep inside you don't know whether to set up a memorial or buy an urn for the ashes. The craziness of life *can* be exhilarating. Carpools and bedtime stories *can* be the highlight of life. As long as you know your purpose in the living.

The question to ask is this: am I doing that which I was created to do? Every woman was created for a life of impact. If you are a mother, you were created to raise children. If you are a wife, you were created to share your life with your spouse. A life of impact is a life that has been invested, whether it's invested in the faces around your dinner table, or invested in five thousand faces at a women's conference. This is what you were created for. When you do what you were created to do, you can enjoy living without being over-whelmed by life.

You see, destiny is not a matter of chance; it is a matter of choice. We can only accomplish in proportion to what we attempt; the reason we feel so little is being accomplished is generally that so little is being attempted. Playing it safe can often create the most insecurity.

I now wake up each morning looking forward to what that day will bring. The gratitude I feel sometimes overwhelms even me. I'm thankful that God got my attention in a way I could not ignore. And I am thankful that I came to the place where I realized that God could actually do something through me to make a difference in the lives of others. Because until we realize that, we will never be effective in our homes, in our neighborhoods, or in our corporations.

I will always be in the process of becoming. Even today, there are areas of my life I have yet to find the beauty in; there are areas of growth I desire to see in me, areas of opportunity I desire to pursue. But every day is another chance to move toward that goal. And maybe today will be the day I find beauty in a new way, in a new place, in a part of me that I've never seen before. Walk with us as we discover what it means to be *free to be beautiful.*

PART II

Ordinary Principles...

CHAPTER 4

Becoming

*H*ave you ever had days where you feel more like a commoner than royalty? Most days? Us too. Ever wondered what it would be like to wake up in a palace? Us too. Ever wondered what you'd do if you opened the door to find a gorgeous prince was standing there holding your shoe from Nordstrom's sale rack? We have.

But what if you were a commoner who didn't feel common? What if you were a commoner who lived in a common village, raised common children, married a common man, went to a common PTA meeting, drove to a common job, yet nothing about you felt common at all? In fact, life to you felt rather uncommon. Even rather extraordinary at times. Crazy? Maybe. But possible.

Do you know how we know? Because every day we are experiencing the reality of this in our own lives. True, some days are better than others. Some lessons are harder to learn than others. True, we are a continual work in progress. But we view life through a different lens now. And it is with that discovery that we invite you to walk with us down common halls, through common kitchens, eating common pork chops and enjoying the fact that life is a tremendously fabulous experience.

Through this journey, we're going to show you the steps you can take to free yourself to be truly beautiful. On this journey, we'll deal with some aspects of life that you might already be good at. But you might also come across one or two that would be more enjoyable if you were watching someone else accomplish them. Some will make you feel like royalty, and others will feel like a royal pain. But each one, when truly embraced, will change a common life into a beautiful life.

Here's a glimpse:

LETTING GO OF THE PAST

Have you ever been inside a prison? Ever been allowed only one visitor a month? Ever had really bad food three times a day? Well, if you've allowed your past to rule your life, then you have been in prison, even if you've never heard the clanging of metal doors behind you. Yet this prison holds one advantage. You have the key in your hand. Do you want to unlock the door? We believe you will.

DEFINING BEAUTIFUL VALUES

No matter who you are you have values. Leaders who pledge aid to those in desperate need have values. Mothers who set boundaries for their children to keep them safe have values. Pop stars that provide Super Bowl–halftime "entertainment" have values. Values are our standard of measure. They are the very things in our life that guide our decision-making. And when all is said and done, we are the ones who have to look in the mirror and determine how we've chosen to let them lead us. What will the mirror say of you?

CREATING A BEAUTIFUL ATTITUDE

Don't think attitude matters? Bet you do when the person behind you screams as they honk their horn and shows you their skill at sign language all because you didn't use your turn signal. Attitude matters in others. But sometimes we forget how much attitude matters in us. Few things destroy a beautiful life more than an ugly attitude. Yet, few things create a beautiful life more than a beautiful attitude. Changing your attitude may not be the easiest thing you've ever done, but it will certainly be one of the most rewarding.

THE BEAUTY OF ACCEPTING GRATEFULLY

Have you ever been given half of a sandwich only to realize your lunch partner kept the larger half for himself? Have you ever been thanked in front of a large group of people only to miss it because you were in the restroom? In both of these situations, there's actually something good to be found. In the first, you can be grateful that you have someone to share a sandwich with. And in the second, you can be grateful that your work was appreciated at all. Every action in life will be received one way or the other. You'll find gratitude is easier to come by than you might have thought.

DEVELOPING AND NURTURING
BEAUTIFUL RELATIONSHIPS

Few things in life offer as much long-term satisfaction as strong relationships. When life is being recounted on the front porch swing or reminisced about around a hospital bed, the thing that will matter is the person you're remembering with. And though these relationships take effort, few things in life have a greater return.

RECOGNIZING THE IMPORTANCE OF TODAY

In this world of uncertainty there is one thing that you can count on: today. So why not grab hold of this moment with both hands? Don't let go until you know you've squeezed every last drop from this day. You will never see tomorrow; "it's always a day away." And you've already learned that the past isn't worth holding onto. But today, well, today's a different story. Why don't you see what it has to tell?

PLANNING PERSONAL GROWTH

You mean I need another plan? I've got "just make it through the day" plans. I've got "how to create a meal with nothing but beef and wieners" plan. I've even got a "how to get to bed before the sun comes up" plan. Who wants another plan? We think you will. When you realize that life can be a determined adventure rather than just blundering chaos, you might be glad you chose to hang on with us a little longer.

DISCOVERING THE BEAUTY OF CHANGE

Change is beautiful when someone else has to do it, don't you think? But we've been surprised how well change actually looks on us. We believe you will, too.

MAKING BEAUTIFUL CHOICES

Choices determine destiny. Beautiful choices determine a beautiful destiny. Some will be easier to make than others. Some will require all the determination you can muster. But each one will make you thankful you were brave enough to choose.

GIVING ABUNDANTLY

Few things reveal the depth of who you are more than what you're willing to give. So in this chapter, we challenge you to give more. Fear might make you want to skip right over this chapter. Shoot, you might want to downright avoid it. But please don't. Why? Because no matter what you give, it will never match what will be returned.

BEGINNING A BEAUTIFUL LIFE JOURNEY WITH PURPOSE

We've made a thousand mistakes: burned dinners, washed "dry clean only's," or killed goldfish by feeding them the rabbit's food. But what things do we do on purpose? Nothing deserves purpose more than your life. And if you'll be purposeful in living it, we guarantee you'll enjoy the journey.

FREE TO BE BEAUTIFUL

Every book has to have an ending chapter. This is ours. We believe that as you walk through each chapter of this book, you'll begin to understand how important it is to take this journey and focus on the life you've been created to live. And we bet that by the time you get here, you'll truly be inspired to be *free to be beautiful.*

CHAPTER 5

Letting Go of the Past
PRINCIPLE 1

*I*t's Monday morning. She's determined to make this one different. The laundry beckons from down the hall. But she decides to linger there on the sofa for just one more moment before facing the mayhem of morning rush hour. The remnants of the second cup of coffee have settled in the cup she holds, and her journal rests across her lap. As she looks back over what she's written, a voice inside says, *Let go of the past.*

She lays her head back on the sofa cushion and thinks about what that would mean. But before she knows it, she's fallen asleep and is dreaming. She sees herself walking across an elaborate stage. Her dress is breathtaking, and flashbulbs are exploding all around her. The audience is cheering her name, and the dance music is bringing the whole room to its feet. What is the commotion all about?

Well, the announcer has just declared her, Claire Elizabeth Whoberry, the Queen of the Pillsbury Bake-Off Contest. Her fabulous peanut butter, triple–layer cake has just won this great culinary honor and a whole lot of money! Her eyes are wide. Her heart is pounding. Her smile is stretched from ear to ear. And the entire moment is captured with her words, "My cake? My peanut butter cake? Is this for real?"

She raises her right arm in a commendable attempt at a Miss America wave, and she breathes in deeply, hoping that this moment will stay locked in her memory forever. But suddenly, words from another world beckon: "Mom! Hey mom! I need some oatmeal."

She opens her eyes to see a tiny face staring into hers. The face that brings her back to reality.

"Sure, son," she says. "I'll be there in a minute."

As she heads to the kitchen, she thinks about the dream. She's had it before. She just wishes the pain of reality would go away. *Let the past go, huh? Easier said than done.*

She's entered that contest three years in a row. And three years in a row Pillsbury informed her that though she met all the eligibility rules, the "test kitchen home economists" just didn't feel she was in the top one hundred entries. So, no trip to the competition finals. No chance to wave like a beauty queen. No cash prize and national recognition. No, this Monday morning she is still just an oatmeal-making mama.

"I'm done cooking. No more peanut butter cakes," she screams to the empty room.

A voice from the bedroom responds. "It's only oatmeal, Mom."

Why can't I let this go, she wonders. I once thought I was destined to be a cook. But if it's my destiny, why haven't I *won*? Maybe I'm just not good enough. Maybe I'm just good enough for doing laundry. It's not like I'm trying to achieve world peace. I don't want to be the centerfold for the *Sports Illustrated* swimsuit edition. I just wanted to win a baking contest.

❧

Have you ever had a dream? Is the life you are living a far cry from the life you *thought* you would live? For many of us, life just hasn't turned out like we planned.

Sometimes, we have little or no control over the turn our life has taken. Miscarriages happen. Fathers abandon wives and children. Houses burn down. People get fired. Earthquakes and hurricanes destroy what took years to build. So please know we understand the heartaches and heartbreaks of life.

Sometimes, hurt and pain are the result of our own making. Bad choices lead to dysfunctional relationships. Inappropriate behavior opens the door to painful consequences. Negative attitudes create negative outcomes.

Often, we deal with our current circumstances by focusing on the past. We constantly relive the mistakes and find ourselves bombarded by the same painful emotions over and over.

We cling to the hurts and the disappointments from our past, nurturing them with tears and self-pity until we can't see a way out. You've seen people like this. They live in the land of "used to be." They don't allow tender touches or kind remarks or simple smiles. And their T-shirts all read, "Leave me alone!" Because people who live in the past have the attitude to go along with it. It's easy to see it in others, isn't it? But what about you? It's always more difficult to see what needs to be removed from our own lives.

When we allow the past to define our present, we are nothing more than captives—prisoners with a lifetime sentence. But unlike most jails, we hold the keys to our own freedom.

Now, we're not doctors, nor do we play them on TV, but we do feel that through our own battles to let go of the past, we have learned some valuable lessons that will help you to use the keys in your hands to release yourself from prison.

DECIDE TO LET GO

If you learn anything from our stories, learn this. For every failure, for every heartache, for every moment of the past that tormented us, God's grace was always there. With a tender nudge, God invited us to be *free to be beautiful.* And not just for our own sake, but if we may be so bold, for the world as well. He came because He loved the world. He loves you and He invites you today, because of that simple truth, to be *free to be beautiful.*

We understand that the thoughts, feelings, and fears that often accompany a painful past may never go away. But as long as you breathe you have a choice about how you respond to those injustices in your life. And your response to those events will either keep you bound or lead you to freedom.

If you *choose* to stay in your prison—while holding your own keys—you will:

- Concentrate only on what you don't have or can't do.

- Hide yourself away.

- Dwell on past experiences and constantly relive the pain.

- Believe that there is no one you can trust.

- Focus on the why's and what if's.

- Yearn for the "good ol' days," while today slips away.

- Develop an attitude and lifestyle of bitterness.

Is this really a life anyone would choose? Maybe not consciously, but many of us choose it every day. We follow our emotions as if by default. But as you'll see, a single choice can change everything.

Tina says:

I wrestle with staying at a healthy weight for my height. Okay, I'll be honest; it's a downright daily battle. And often, because of my past failings, I feel like simply giving up forever. But what will that gain? Nothing but more weight! When I give up, *I'm* the loser and I'm not talking about pounds and inches. However, on the days when I make the decision to focus on what I know to be true and let go of the fear of failing, I'm able to stop beating myself up. And I become free to achieve the very dream I desire. ◊

What do the years of beating ourselves accomplish? Nothing but bruises. Have you ever had a bruise? There's nothing attractive about it. And if you hit yourself in the same spot again, you feel the pain even more deeply than the first time. And when you're in pain, it's not easy to have a good attitude. Eventually, those around us get tired of our constant bitterness and bad moods, and before too long, begin to retreat.

But what if, rather than bumping those past bruises, we choose to do something to help them heal? What if we take action *against* our past? How do we do it?

The first step is to tell God all about it. The only way to start letting go of the pain is to be completely honest before God.

Once you release your mistakes and your regrets, you will be free to press on toward the purpose for which you were created.

Let go of the fear that says, "I can't" and find freedom in the faith that *you can.*

- You can let go of your past disappointments and gain a clearer perspective of your future.

- You can seek forgiveness and then receive it.

- You can forgive yourself and then forgive others.

- You can wake up today with the right attitude and a renewed commitment to be in a right relationship with your Maker, others, and yourself.

- You can realize the importance of today and let go of disappointments by regaining a proper perspective to reach your goals and dreams.

- You can let go of fear and be liberated in faith.

- You can ask for and receive forgiveness for yourself.

Dan Sullivan, in his book, *Focusing on Your Unique Ability,* says that we are all made up of three separate "selves." The *past self* is the person we think we've been up until now. The *future self* is the person we think we will become in the coming years. And the *present self* is the person we think we are right now. However, the *present self* is really a composite of the two other selves.[3] In other words, the person you think you are now is a combination of who you think you've been and who you think you'll become.

This is where each person differs. Each of us has made a different commitment of time to our past and our future. If you spend more time wallowing in your past, trying to change something that is already a permanent fixture, you show that what has already happened to you is more important than anything that lies ahead. People who are committed to their past selves become frozen in a past image of themselves and as a result, become conventional and predictable in their thoughts and actions. On the other hand, a commitment to your *future you* indicates that what lies ahead is more meaningful than any of your memories. And your unique abilities lie in your *vision of who you will become.*

You can't change the past but you can change the future.

"You make it sound so easy," you might say. "But you don't know my track record." Well, we may not know yours, but trust us, we know our own. When you realize that you can simply turn around from your mistakes and run in the direction of your determination, you're ready to move to the next stage.

So how do you move from the past to the future? Begin by thinking about your dream. We suggest you do it aloud so you can hear it for yourself. Then you need to affirm that dream through action. You can do this by offering a prayer of thanksgiving for what you can become. Then, be patient and watch as each day that you learn to let go of the past you grow more and more *free . . .* and more and more *beautiful.* We believe that when you let go of the past, you'll have more energy to be persistent in the pursuit of your dream.

This was certainly the case for Ms. Pillsbury Baker. Rather than concentrating on her past failed attempts, she turned her eyes toward the future and her goal of winning that contest. She tested recipes and worked to perfect them as often as she could. And while she has not yet won the prize, she has once again found the joy and freedom in dreaming.

We offer it to you like this: neither of us have it all together. But we do strive daily to keep our eye on the goals that are before us. And we have determined that no matter the obstacles, no matter the journey, we're in this for the long haul. Turning back isn't an option.

CHAPTER 6

Defining Beautiful Values
PRINCIPLE 2

The Woman in the Mirror

When you get what you want in your struggle for self

And the world crowns you "Queen for a Day"

Just go to the mirror and look at yourself

And see what that one has to say

For it isn't your father or mother or sister or brother

Whose judgment upon you must pass

The person whose verdict counts most in your life

Is the one staring back from the glass

You may be like Jack Horner and chisel a plum

And think you're a wonderful gal

But the gal in the glass says you're only a bum

If you can't look her straight in the eye

She's the one to please, never mind all the rest

You've passed your most dangerous, difficult test

When the gal in the glass is your friend

You can fool the whole world down your pathway of years

And get pats on the back as you pass

But your final reward will be heartache and tears

If you've cheated the one in the glass.[4]

No matter who you are, you have values. Leaders who pledge aid to those in desperate need have values. Mothers who set boundaries for their children to keep them safe have values. Even drug dealers who ensnare our children have values. Pop stars that provide Super Bowl–halftime "entertainment" have values. Values are our standard of measure. They are the standards in our life that guide our decision-making. And when all is said and done, we are the ones who have to look in the mirror and determine how we've chosen to let them lead us.

Many people live their life with less than beautiful values. They make poor decisions and often bring hurt to themselves and to those around them. But when you take into consideration the many factors that form a person's values, it really shouldn't come as much of a surprise. Our values are based on our family environment, our fortune or our misfortune, our religious beliefs or lack thereof. Values are the ideas we have about what is good and what is bad, and how things should be. They are the fundamental beliefs that drive our behavior and our decision-making. But when your life is written, your character won't be measured by your successful accomplishments, but by the person that you were, the values by which you lived. We can't be *free to be beautiful* if we are trapped by less-than–beautiful values. The goal in each of our lives should be to develop the kind of values that windy days can't blow away. Our values must become the very things that hold us steady, no matter where the rest of the world may blow.

❧

To truly understand what changes you may need to make in your value system, it's important to take stock in where you are. Most of us truly desire to live by beautiful values. We want to live with integrity and consistency. And most of us do our best to live this way every day. But life is tough. Of that, there is no doubt. Values must become our foundation if we want to be *free to be beautiful.*

To truly be free you have to be grounded, grounded in both who you are and in what you believe. The following steps will help you to begin the process of defining beautiful values in your life. First, take out a piece of paper and pen and find a quiet place where you can concentrate.

Start by creating a list of your values—the beliefs and ideas that mean the most to you. Some examples might include accuracy, reliability, strength, loyalty, fun, peace, safety, commitment, and equality.

Once you've created a list of your own personal values, determine where they fit into the different categories of your life. (Some may fall in more than one area.) Some of the areas in your life may include: spiritual, service, attitude, love, finances, career, community, personal growth, relationships, family, recreation, generosity, or health.

Next, ask yourself the following questions about each value:

- Is this a "beautiful" value? Why or why not?

- What is my personal definition of this value?

- How can I be sure that this value is displayed in my own life?

- What people do I know whose lives reflect this value?

- What is my strategy for implementing this value in my life?
- How can I be intentional about practicing this value in my life?
- How will I make this value a priority in my life today?
- How can this value be a benefit in my life?

Keep the answers to these questions with you for a couple of months. Think about them and look at them as often as you can as you go through your day. And when you're facing a decision or a difficult circumstance, pull the paper out and measure your choices and decisions against your values.

Why is it so important to go to all this trouble? Because a truly beautiful life isn't possible without defining, embracing, and sometimes even changing the value system that guides you.

 Karen says:

Tina and I believe in an "ultimate" mirror. We stand together in the fact that the one and only measure of true character and integrity is God's Word. You may think this is an odd way of viewing life. But we have discovered it is the *only* way to view life in its intended form. And if you long to look in the mirror at the end of the day and truly know that you have "cheated" no one, God's Word is the place to begin. ❧

Strive not to be a success, but rather to be of value.

~ ALBERT EINSTEIN

Recently, the local news reported a story about a tourist who was passing through Nashville as he headed to spend the holidays somewhere else. In his hurry to get on the road, he forgot his wallet in his hotel room. When the hotel maid found the wallet, she opened it to try to find an address for the owner and discovered eight thousand dollars in cash inside. She called the manager, who called the owner. And when the owner arrived back at the hotel every single item was still in his wallet, including every last dollar.

It would have been easy for the woman to take the money. She certainly needed it. Times had been tough lately and the money would have made things better. Who would know? She could have said she never saw it, stashed it away, and enjoyed herself for a little while. But she didn't. And do you know what happened? The owner of the wallet gave her three thousand dollars for her honesty. She shared with the reporter how grateful she was for what the gentleman had given her.

But this woman had far more than money. She had character that stood the test. Her values guided her in this situation, but had she not determined them before that day, she may have made an entirely differ-ent decision. She lived by a set of values that made her a woman worth far more than three thousand dollars.

How do you feel when you hear that kind of story? Doesn't that encourage you to reflect on your own values? As you take the time to discover what your values already are, what values you want to instill in your life, and what steps you need to take to create the type of values you long to have, you'll be laying a solid foundation and freeing yourself to live a beautiful life.

Do we dare bring up another fairy tale? Oh, why not! In Dave Ramsey's book *More than Enough*, he offers what he calls the "Three Little Pigs Principle."[5] Do you remember the story of the three little pigs?

One little pig built his house out of straw because—well, he was cheap. The second pig built his house out of sticks because sticks were easily obtained, easy to work with, and easy to throw up on the house. The third little pig spent more effort and certainly more money and built his house out of brick.

The first two little pigs lost their homes when the big bad wolf came huffing and puffing. But the third little pig outlasted all of the wolf's antics because his foundation was strong enough to endure everything the wolf had to offer. It must have dawned on the other two pigs that the wolf was always waiting around the corner to "huff and puff" because they headed over to Pig Three's house every Monday night at seven to take "Brick Building 101." They figured he could probably teach them a thing or two. Why not? He was the only one living a beautiful life.

All in all . . . we're certain they lived happily ever after.

CHAPTER 7

Creating a Beautiful Attitude
PRINCIPLE 3

*E*ver had a bad hair day? Ever woke up to find your attitude
matches your hair? Nothing seems to go right. The children forget
their lunches, the last one to drive the car thought it would run
on fumes, and your coworkers forgot to let you know that casual
Friday wasn't casual anymore. With each event, you become more
and more frustrated until you finally just give up. And by this time,
your attitude is downright unpleasant.

Attitude is affected by the actions of others and your response
to those actions. And unfortunately, attitudes are like undergarments.
Sometimes they're showing, and people are reluctant to tell you!
But the area of attitude is critical when it comes to personal growth.

More than anything else, attitude determines success in life.

Karen says:

Not too long ago, I was standing in a hotel lobby waiting for the elevator. As with most people, my mind was elsewhere. I was mentally preparing for a rather important presentation that I was excited about giving. I was going to be speaking to a group of people that I really admired, so my spirits were excited with the anticipation of what I was about to do.

The elevator door opened and I stepped inside, right into the Land of Whining, Complaining, and downright Disgusting Attitudes that I was "privileged" to enjoy for eleven floors. Even those not participating in the loathsome chatter carried expressions just as sour.

As I stepped off feeling "yuck," I realized immediately that a group of people I did not know—and at that moment had no desire to know—had just impacted my attitude in no more than an elevator trip. Only eleven floors earlier I had been a rather happy woman. Now, I was feeling discouraged. It took a few minutes of self-talk and personal affirmation to place my spirits back on their original floor: excited.

But watch out for me now if I get on your elevator because, since that day, I step into them differently. I enter smiling and just as the doors close, I announce that it is a beautiful day, regardless of the weather outside. Then, I pick at least one person on that elevator to compliment. Now who's in control of the elevator? Me. And I've discovered that when I do this, most people leave the elevator smiling and encouraged about their day. What a difference an attitude and an elevator can make! ❧

If we are truly honest with ourselves, we will realize that attitude is the difference-maker in life. It dictates whether you are living life or life is living you. It determines whether you are *on* your way or *in* your way. And more than anything else, your attitude determines your success. Why? Because it affects every area of your life as well as the lives of those around you. Just as you can set the tone for your day by your attitude, you can also set the tone for someone else's day. And if you don't believe that, take a trip on an elevator.

In order for you to get the most from this chapter, take a moment to evaluate your present attitude. The goal isn't for you to determine what is wrong with you, but instead to uncover what is wrong with your attitude so that you can be *free to be beautiful.*

First, take an honest look at your life and truly evaluate those feelings that tend to consume you when "life" happens. When faced with difficult circumstances, how do you tend to react? Do you immediately think the worst or do you search for the silver lining? Do you say to yourself, *Why me?* Or do you take the time to count your blessings?

As you evaluate these attitudes, think about their source. Are they rooted in past experiences or old hurts? If so, go back to chapter 5 and work through the steps of letting go of your past.

Next, take some time to study your thought patterns. What do you think about over the course of a day? What do these thoughts say to you? Are they positive or negative?

Finally, look at the behavior that this kind of thinking leads to. If your feelings and thoughts prompt you to help people rise to what they were created for, you might be better off than you think. But if your attitudes and actions tend to deplete the joy of those around you, then this is an area of your life that truly needs to be addressed. Do yourself and those you love a favor, and make a commitment to address your negative attitudes. Don't wait for someone to have to tell you your slip is showing. Take an honest look at yourself in the mirror before you spend your day with others and attend to the things that need attention.

John C. Maxwell gives this perspective on "What is an Attitude?" from his book, *The Winning Attitude.*

> It is the "advance [woman]" of our true selves.
> Its roots are inward but its fruit is outward.
> It is our best friend or our worst enemy.
> It is more honest and more consistent than our words.
> It is an outward look based on past experiences.
> It is a thing, which draws people to us or repels them.
> It is never content until it is expressed.
> It is the librarian of our past.
> It is the speaker of our present.
> It is the prophet of our future.[6]

Even a beautiful woman has days when she isn't, well, beautiful. It's the morning that a "series of unfortunate events" arrives on her doorstep all at once. We all have them. But an *attitude* that has become an unfortunate event in and of itself very often becomes the filter through which that person views life. A negative attitude usually stems from one of these areas: regret, resentment, resistance, or rejection. Regret and resentment are *inside* issues. Resistance and rejection are *outside* issues.

And each one of these, when they have become a way of life, can affect our perception of ourselves and the world around us, making us anything but free, and anything but beautiful.

But if we can learn to deal with these four areas, we're one step closer to freedom.

THE FALLOUT OF REGRET

Regret is an appalling waste of energy: you can't build on it;
it's only good for wallowing in.
~ KATHERINE MANSFIELD

Regret finds its way to us through a multitude of avenues: unfulfilled dreams, unmet expectations, wasted efforts, or past mistakes. Regret can become all-consuming, and eventually, if not dealt with, extremely destructive. Regret uses self-doubt, guilt, and self-pity to convince us that we are not worthy. Regret targets the subconscious and wreaks havoc on our self-image, leaving us with a perception of beauty that is flawed and broken.

Self-Doubt is one of the harshest end results of regret. It creates a feeling of inadequacy. For self-doubters, life becomes nothing more than a game of comparison. And we're the ones who always fall short. When we play the comparison game, we are comparing our worst to someone else's best. It's a game we will never win. You will always fall short. And this perspective can lead to a toxic attitude.

Guilt is another result of regret and a common comrade of many. Some live in guilt based on mistakes of the past. A moment of poor choice or patterns of bad behavior have brought them to a place where they live in constant guilt over something that can never be undone. Some live in guilt on a daily basis for nothing bigger than forgetting to pack a lunch or missing a carpool. Guilt is a toxic attitude that has also been discovered to be toxic to your body.

Combined studies at Harvard, the University of Michigan, and Dartmouth College suggest that the psychological effects of prolonged self-blame and guilt are cumulative, with rapid physical deterioration becoming obvious around age forty-five.

Self-Pity is another by-product of regret and one of the most unattractive attitudes one can possess. It is often brought on by the need for attention. Many times, people fall into a state of self-pity because their need for attention has not been met. But their failure to receive attention could be a result of the unattractive way in which they strive for it and the attitude they exhibit. Self-pity makes for a lonely companion.

THE IMPORTANCE OF OUR RESPONSE

Meet a person with a beautiful attitude and you will realize it is a result of the way she perceives life and responds to failure. The most beautiful way to respond to life is with an attitude of acceptance. Life happens; it always will. Just as life happened today, it is sure to show up again tomorrow. Some of your choices will make you want to slap yourself. Others, you'll want to share with the world. But unless you accept the circumstances you currently have and look forward to creating new circumstances, you'll continue to live in the same cycle of destruction.

Mistakes of the past only determine our future when we allow them to. And gaining a proper perspective of those mistakes is the key to developing a beautiful attitude. In a life where you take two steps back for every three steps forward, you can see it one of two ways: Life keeps slapping you backward, or with each adjustment, you're gaining a step.

Have you ever walked into a hospital room and seen the monitor that reveals a person's heart rate? If all is going well, the line jumps up with each beat of the heart to create peaks and valleys. Often in life we want to avoid the peaks and valleys. Even though the highs can be very high, the lows don't seem to be worth the price. So we would prefer just a flat line, a normal life where everything stays the same and runs at a consistent place. But in case you've forgotten, flat is dead. The ups and downs of life are what create the existence of life at all.

You see, it's not the act of failing that's the issue. Most of us have become experts at that, anyway. No, it is the attitude we have about our failures that makes the difference in life. Avoiding failure altogether will simply leave you dead and lifeless. And a person is free to be beautiful when she realizes that failure isn't the worst life has to offer.

Tina says:

Recently, I came across this story about a man who buried his money. His boss had gone off on an extended trip. He called his employees together and told them he had some responsibilities to delegate to them while he was gone. So he handed the first employee a check for five thousand dollars. To the next one he gave a check for two thousand dollars. And to the third, he gave a check for one thousand dollars. (Each amount was a reflection of their abilities.) Then he left.

No sooner had the boss gone out the door when the first one with five thousand dollars got to work. He made calls, he made deals, and before he knew it, his five thousand had turned into ten thousand. The second man did the same thing. And soon his two thousand dollars grew to four thousand. But the third one—well, he had a different perspective. He went outside, walked around to the back of the office where he dug a hole in a grassy patch underneath. Then he buried his thousand dollars.

When the boss came back, he wanted to know what the men had done with their money. The first one showed what he had accomplished. The boss looked at him and said, "You have done an excellent job. If you can do that with five thousand dollars, show me what you can do with ten." And in one moment the employee's money was doubled a second time.

The second man showed what he had accomplished. And the boss bestowed the same accolades and the same reward, giving him another two thousand dollars.

Then came the third man. "Uh, sir, I have some good news and some bad news. Bad news first. I know that you demand excellence and have strong requirements. Truth be told, you scare me a little, and I didn't want to lose your money. So I buried it. The good news is I still have every penny."

Puzzled, the boss looked at him. Then he said, "You lazy man. The least you could have done would be to put it in an interest–bearing account and gotten me some kind of return. So, since you weren't even willing to do that, then take your check and hand it to the man with ten thousand dollars. And after you've done that, pack your bags and don't plan on returning."[7]

What struck me as I read this story was the difference in the attitudes of these three men. They were all in the same environment and were all given the same task: take care of this money. But their perspectives were quite different. You could reason a number of possibilities for the third man's actions, but the one thing you can't deny is that his fear of failing was ultimately what brought about even greater failure. Often we try to avoid failure only to come face to face with it in even greater ways and with far more lasting results.

So did this man learn anything after he left? We'll never know. But he could have. If he were wise, he would have taken that failure and let it forever change his character.

Truth be told, winning and succeeding can reveal aspects of who we are, but nothing reveals our true character more than when we fail. And if allowed, failure can actually help us to grow in areas of our life that we have formerly neglected. ❧

Though you cannot go back and make a brand new start, my friend,
anyone can start from now and make a brand new end.

~ UNKNOWN

THE FACE OF RESENTMENT

Have you ever noticed how that chip on your shoulder can become
a heavy load? Few things affect an attitude like resentment. When
asked to explain the lack of great statesmen in the world, Napoleon
said, "To get to power you need to display absolute pettiness; to
exercise power you need to show true greatness; such pettiness and
such greatness are rarely found in one human being." And since we're
being honest, jealousy is one of the prime measures of resentment,
as well as the tribute the mediocre pay to achievers.

Let's face it. There is nothing beautiful about resentment. In fact,
resentment can be life damaging. It will hurt us far more than it will
hurt the one we resent. It also causes us to focus on the wrong things
instead of the things we have been called to accomplish. Resentment
completely drains us of the energy we need to perform the things we
have been called to do. And then it leaves us with a negative attitude
so entrenched that it can take years and great effort to transform.

So, what do we do with this great negative emotion? As with anything in life that we desire to change, we have to *admit* that we need
to change in the first place. Then we need to evaluate the cause and
effect, to identify the "who" or the "why." Who do we resent and why
do we resent that person? Once you've determined the source of your
resentment, you can begin to make adjustments to your perspective.
How can you take your current resentments and turn them into something positive? Are you angry because your gymnastic career never took
off like Mary Lou Retton's? Are you jealous of her gold medals when all

you have are a few pieces of gold-plated jewelry? The best way to change your perspective is to be honest. Acknowledge and accept your own limitations, as well as the limitations of others. Finally, set some new goals for yourself that are doable in light of the time, abilities, and resources available to you.

THE FRUSTRATION OF RESISTANCE

Resistance is a common roadblock to success. And we usually hit it just about the time we feel we're making progress on the path to being *free to be beautiful.* Sometimes the very source of resistance will be you. That's the reason we wrote this book. But at other times, it will come from those around you.

Unfortunately, not everyone enjoys the progress of others. Simply put, motion causes friction. You wouldn't think those who love you would want you to stay in attitudes that were less than beautiful, but often people grow accustomed to your face, as the old song goes from *My Fair Lady.*

And it could be that as you are becoming more beautiful and "alive," those around you realize how "dead" they feel. So in order for them to remain comfortable, they want you to remain the same. It could also be that they simply don't understand why you want to change. Don't let resistance cause you to retreat. Instead, use it to keep yourself honest. Let your loved ones know what you're trying to accomplish.

> *People will support what they help to create.*
> ~ MARY KAY ASH

Many times in our personal businesses, we observe women dealing with resistance to new endeavors. Most of the time it's those closest to them who are the most discouraging because they may feel threatened by the changes that have occurred. And since women tend to be wired to put themselves last on the priority list, this resistance often results in the loss of their dreams. This is a shame, because ultimately, a change in attitude could benefit everyone.

 Karen says:

Early in my business I made a decision that if I was going to leave my job as a teacher and give my heart to this new business, I was going to have to reach higher and work harder to accomplish something I had never accomplished before. This meant I would have to do things that I had never done before. It would require more travel and less time at home. But I saw it as "short-term pain" necessary to accomplish a "long-term gain."

So, knowing we could all benefit from this new opportunity, our family sat down together. We discussed the changes that would take place and the reasons each was necessary. We discussed how these changes would affect us. Then, we talked about the long-term benefits and shared rewards that these changes would offer us. We decided that when we met our goal, the immediate reward would be a world-class trip to Germany for the entire family!

By the time we were finished talking, everyone was excited about where we were headed and what their part in the goal was. There were many times that year we questioned if the changes in our lives were worth it. Then, we would remind ourselves of the rewards. And when business required me to miss a ballgame or not participate in a school activity, I always thanked my family for their sacrifices and made sure to reward them with small extras along the way. The fact that we made this plan together allowed everyone to value his part in achieving the goal.

Resistance tends to weaken once people realize that change is a nonnegotiable. People around you may test the limits; they may challenge you to see just how serious you are. You must be resolute and never waiver in your resolve to improve your attitude. Be obvious and passionate in your journey, sharing your *progress* not your *problems*. There's no better day to begin than today!

THE FOLLY OF REJECTION

For some people, rejection has become a way of life. They received it at home, found it at school, and experienced it again when they got married. For others, rejection is a new experience: the spouse that abandoned them, the company that discarded them, or the friend that turned against them. Either way, the wounds of rejection are raw and real. And when you are rejected, you can't help but remember every other time you've been abandoned in your life. We all experience rejection at one time or another. How will you respond when it happens to you?

Women especially have a difficult time dealing with rejection. When we feel rejected, it's awfully tough to feel beautiful. But when you learn to cope with rejection, you will find the freedom you need to feel truly beautiful.

Dealing with rejection begins with a healthy perspective on the subject, realizing that your perception of a situation might not be what was originally intended. Few people *intend* to reject someone else. But often when we feel like we've been rejected, we've actually misinterpreted someone's original intent. So it's important that we guard against the tendency to view every situation as potential rejection. We need to actively press the "pause" button in moments when rejection would try to crush us and determine if that was the motive of the individual. If we don't, it will be a continual cycle.

So how do we avoid that familiar pitfall? You know who you really are, and you know that you *are* worthy. Affirm yourself: the woman in the mirror may not look totally fabulous at six a.m., but wait until they see her at eight! Affirm your beliefs: as a daughter of the King, you belong to the One who will never reject you. Affirm your values: Beautiful values flow to create a beautiful life, one that is worthy and filled with possibility.

Then don't be afraid to do what is right for you. Successful people do what unsuccessful people won't do.

Thoughts of a Beautiful Lady

People are unreasonable, illogical, and self centered;

Love them anyway.

If you are kind, people may accuse you of selfish ulterior motives;

Be kind anyway.

If you are successful, you will win false friends and true enemies;

Succeed anyway.

If you are honest and frank, people may cheat you;

Be honest anyway.

What you spend years building, someone could destroy overnight;

Build anyway.

If you find serenity and happiness, they may be jealous;

Be happy anyway.

The good you do today people will often forget;

Do good anyway.

Give the world the best you have and it may never be enough;

Give the world the best you've got anyway.

You see, in the final analysis it is between you and God;

it was never between you and them anyway. [8]

~ MOTHER TERESA

Attitude is simply our outlook on life. Often we find ourselves
so focused on the challenges that we allow the blessings to pass
by unnoticed. Sometimes, simply determining to catch them and
appreciate them will completely change our perspective. A beautiful
attitude focuses on the possibilities rather than the problems and
is essential to an abundant life.

The greatest challenge in developing a beautiful attitude is making
it part of our daily routine. Attitudes quickly revert to their original
patterns if not carefully guarded. Truly beautiful people know that
the inside is just as important as what is on the outside. And when we
begin to see ourselves as beautiful, the world will view us the same way.

**One of your greatest weapons against your attitude
will be how you respond to yourself.**

We can destroy our own attitude daily with our internal conversation. We can limit ourselves because of the negative way we talk
to ourselves. But self-talk can have the opposite effect as well.
We can create a beautiful attitude daily simply by focusing our
internal conversations on things that are positive and beautiful.
If we learn how to do this well, we can change even the most
unattractive attitudes.

Self-Talk is that little incessant voice we listen to all day long.
As children we just said things out loud. Everything that came through
our thoughts usually ran right out through our mouth. But as adults,
we have learned to keep those thoughts to ourselves. And as the tape

plays in our head, it programs our subconscious mind. However, our subconscious mind cannot tell the difference between a truth and a lie as it programs our conscious mind. The danger in this is that, for many of us, our self-talk has been rooted in old ways of thinking that have created unhealthy and unproductive ways of living. Yet once we change those old behaviors, this is one of the primary areas that we will daily have to approach with a different attitude.

Think back to this morning. You woke up and walked to the bathroom mirror. What were your first thoughts? *Oh, don't I look fabulous! Who can stand me? My forehead has no wrinkles and my complexion is like a baby's.* Or maybe you woke up, looked in the mirror, it screamed, and you screamed back. *How is it that I can go to bed looking like a human and wake up looking like a science project? I'm certain my face gained five pounds overnight. Oh, well, it may take a while but I'll look as decent as possible by the time I leave. I better get started before I'm late.*

Who could complain about either voice? Granted, the first voice isn't as likely as the second. It could, in fact, be downright denial, but it is how each of us longs to see ourselves. But both affirmations will affect your attitude. Affirmation gives you the capability to control your destiny through your most powerful component: yourself!

An affirming life is a beautiful life. And affirmation contains the priceless elements of your belief, your attitude, and your motivation, using words charged with power, conviction, and faith.

Every day, make an effort to affirm yourself. Repeat it until it gets into your heart. Visualize it until it gets into your mind. Believe it until it changes your very life.

Repetition is important in affirmation. It sends a positive response to your subconscious, which, as we discussed, accepts whatever you tell it as truth. And when you have done this, it then triggers positive feelings that in turn drive action and attraction. And you become attracted to the very attitude you are trying to achieve. Then, when you visualize it in your mind, you are that much closer to achieving it in your life. Affirmation gets on the inside of you and stirs up those beliefs that you had let die or simply refused to believe. And when they are allowed to return to life, your strengths become maximized, your weaknesses become minimized, and your potential is unleashed.

Each one of us, if we truly looked at ourselves honestly and objectively, would admit that our attitude is a reflection of our personal outlook on life. If our outlook is pessimistic, then our attitude will follow. We will find ourselves moody, depressed, and looking for the cloud instead of the rainbow. But if our outlook on life is optimistic, we will be peaceful, happy, and pointing out rainbows even in the midst of the storm.

Anyone can change an attitude. It simply takes a determined effort. It requires us to focus on our blessings and look at life as a world of possibilities instead of squandered moments. This is the kind of attitude that will free us to live a beautiful and abundant life. Taking an active role in turning the negative aspects of your life into positives and recognizing opportunity is an easy way to begin the change in your attitude and your actions.

Instead of wanting to do bodily harm to the little munchkin who forgot his lunch for the fifth time in a five-day week, look at it as an opportunity to get to see him one more time during the day. Instead of being embarrassed and frustrated at work because no one told you it wasn't casual Friday anymore, use your lunch break to buy that great outfit you have been eyeing. And when you want to wring someone's neck for leaving your car on empty, instead realize that those extra minutes sitting at the gas pump might have been the very moments you needed to avoid a car accident.

**Every moment offers you total control over its
enjoyment or its stress.**

So take all the time you need. And know that maintaining a positive attitude in *all* areas of life is never truly complete. But as long as we breathe, we have the ability and the need to try. Very often people think that a new way of thinking is a result of a new attitude, but in fact, a new attitude is really a result of a new way of thinking.

Nothing in life is more difficult than changing outward actions. But it is impossible without changing inward feelings. So take a moment and look in the mirror and affirm yourself: You are deeply loved, deeply valued, intricately designed, and magnificently cared for. Now let this beautiful attitude free you to live a beautiful life. Because a beautiful life is a reflection of a beautiful spirit, which has been cultivated by a beautiful attitude. And to truly be beautiful we must realize that the journey can be as enjoyable as the destination.

CHAPTER 8

Accepting Gratefully
PRINCIPLE 4

Tina says:

Some friends of mine inherited a small sum of money after their father's death. Their frustration was revealed when they said, "Can you believe this is all he left us?" They felt like it was some cruel joke. Through the years they had described their life to me. Their family had lived in poverty, and financial worries just seemed to be an old wound that wouldn't heal. My friends wanted this "cycle" of the past to be broken, however, because they didn't want this to become a way of life for their own children.

But as they spoke that day, my heart was grieved at their view of this moment in life. Their words were filled with emotion. But gratitude wasn't among them. Not a snippet of, "Gee, we lived so poor as a family, isn't it a miracle that anything was left for us at all? Can you believe that in our father's inability to provide all those years, he found four hundred and fifty dollars to leave us now? What a blessing! We bet this was something he had dreamed about ever since we were little."

On any path to freedom there is one attribute that needs to accompany the journey: gratitude. We love it when others are grateful for what we've done: "Mom, the broccoli was fabulous." You know your child hates broccoli. But his grateful attitude changes the very atmosphere of your home.

So why is it so hard to live a life of gratitude when we know how receiving gratitude makes us feel? We also know that when we don't receive gratitude for something we've worked hard at, it's easy to have an ugly attitude. And if we've learned anything yet, we know that *attitude* affects everything. That's why we suggest an attitude of gratitude in your journey toward freedom.

There's a story in the Bible about ten lepers. They were hanging out by themselves one day, because that's what lepers did. They called to Jesus and asked Him to have mercy on them. He did. He healed each one of them. But listen to this: Only one came back to say thank you. Even Jesus said, "Did I miss something here, or didn't I heal ten of you? Where are the other nine?"[9]

We never find out. All we know is that only one had a heart of gratitude. Maybe the others were just self-focused. Did they think Jesus had a personal relief program to leper colonies? No matter what they thought, they didn't come back. Would you? ❧

You know what tends to happen when a person discovers the beauty in gratitude? She starts looking for ways to express it. Even sitting here writing this today, in our comfortable chairs in our comfortable homes, we are reminded of how we can express it ourselves.

- It can be with a "thank you."
- It can be with a kind word.
- It can be with our time.
- It can be with our unconditional love.
- It can be with sharing what we've learned from
  our own experiences.
- It can be through a prayer of gratitude.
- It can be through our resources.
- It can be through our support.
- It can be from Tiffany's!
- It can be through the touch of hand or a hug around a neck.

MIRROR, MIRROR ON THE WALL . . .

Do you remember the queen in the story of Snow White? We think we've figured out why she had such serious self-esteem issues, which ultimately led to that evil apple. Every day she looked in the mirror and asked, "Mirror, mirror, on the wall, who's the fairest one of all?" And the mirror always had a response: the queen was the fairest. But one day "Miss Queen" got a wake-up call. Someone more beautiful had arrived. Snow White was in town and "Miss Thang"—oops, "Miss Queen" wasn't all *that* anymore.

The only option the queen saw was to destroy Snow White so the mirror would declare her once again as the "fairest of them all." Has this ever happened to you? Have you ever found out someone could sing better than you? Or someone really could make a better peanut butter cake? Or someone looked better in that outfit than you? It happens to all of us.

Our mirror shrieks at us, "Child, seen your boobs lately? Well your knees have a great view of them. Checked out your thighs? If they spread any farther you're going to have to go to the wide angled mirror. And your face, well, I don't think you can take much more."

We get this response because we're looking in the *wrong mirror.* There's only one place where your true identity can be found: in the One who made you. There's no mirror more honest than the Word of God. What if the queen had gone to a mirror that told her she was uniquely made and perfect the way she was? What if she had been grateful for the way she was instead of longing to be someone else? The whole story would have been different.

It's time to rewrite your story as well. Turn off the TV shows that tell you you'd be better off if your nose were smaller or your boobs were bigger. Close the magazines that declare unless you're emaciated you're unhealthy. And open up a mirror that tells you the truth. You are fearfully and wonderfully made. You are loved, and you were created to serve and to be free . . . *free to be beautiful.*

 Karen says:

At the age of forty-eight and at one of the most successful times in my father's career, he suffered a heart attack. After a quadruple bypass and thirty-seven days in the hospital, my father was finally sent home. Because of his long and painful recovery, his business suffered. When he was finally able to get back to work, the stamina he had once known wasn't what it used to be. So he simply came to terms with it, restructured his business, and began to enjoy the success he did have during this new season of his life.

Eight years later, he began to experience chest pains once again. While the doctors were evaluating him, he suffered a violent heart attack, and they rushed him to emergency surgery. The heart attacks continued even on the operating table. And during the twelve-hour operation, the surgeon had to revive my dad seven times. When the doctor came out, he told us how "sick" my dad's heart truly was and that we should prepare ourselves for the worst.

That precious surgeon, whom we labeled our "angel," spent all night with my father in his recovery room. And at four different times, he again revived my father. That hospitalization lasted for three months. He spent both Thanksgiving and Christmas there, but it didn't matter. They were probably the most special and memorable holidays we've ever had.

Because his heart was so sick, they implanted a balloon pump in it. Usually this device is left in no longer than twelve hours, but dad had to have it for more than seventy-two hours. The repercussions of that extended period resulted in the loss of both of his legs. The day they amputated my father's legs was probably one of the most agonizing and heart breaking days of my life. And I'm certain it was for him as well. Most of the people who knew him were sure he would give up on life after this. My dad had always had a pretty strong ego, and had really maintained a physically active lifestyle. So, all I could do was trust that something good would reveal itself and he would find a reason to fight.

He shocked us all. He decided to close his business and make his therapy his new "job." He set out to encourage his therapists and the other patients. He counseled those who were afraid of going into surgery. And he always told each one of them to "just take a risk on life." He amazed us all.

Then one day, my doorbell rang. And on the other side was my father, *standing*. He had driven four hours and arrived with a look of pride on his face. He had mastered his prosthesis and wanted to take his daughter and grandchildren for a walk. It was the *best* walk I've ever taken.

Disability was just a label to my dad, not a lifestyle. He cooked dinner on Wednesday nights for the church. He was involved in all kinds of activities in the community. He worked the polls during elections. He refined his cooking skills. And he took guitar lessons, making music that could make others happy, something he had always wanted to do. He made time for his buddies. He couldn't golf with them anymore, but he could have lunch. And they did most every week, these buddies from high school days. Through the years, they shared the ups and downs that go with life: the loss of spouses, terminal cancer, and everything else life threw their way.

And he enjoyed his family—his grandchildren, his children, and my mother. They met at thirteen, got married when they were eighteen, and were soul mates through it all. Even with battles of pneumonia that would kill lesser people, he always seemed to pull through. Then came more news. He needed a heart transplant.

There is an age limit on heart transplants. And he was four months from that limit. We were told it could take up to a year, maybe even longer, to receive an organ. But one day, the call did come.

Two weeks before his birthday that would have removed him from the list, he was sent to Vanderbilt in Nashville and prepped for surgery. "Honey, no matter how it goes, *I win*," he told me. Twenty hours later he became the first double amputee to successfully undergo a heart transplant.

Not one time during any of that experience did I ever hear my father complain, express regret, or wish life away. No, he just gave. And I will never forget what he taught me in the process. ❧

Accepting Gratefully

When we give cheerfully and accept gratefully, everyone is blessed.
~ MAYA ANGELOU

If you are unhappy with your lot in life, build a service station on it.
~ CORRIE TEN BOOM

Gratitude is crucial to happiness. Find something to be grateful for today and then sit back and watch what it will do for you. It will begin to excite your hope and diminish your despair. It will increase your faith and reduce your fear. It will remind you that life is a gift not a right. It will bring your very life into a place of peace and contentment. It will comfort you and refresh you so that you can offer it to someone else. And more than anything, it will allow you to be *free to be beautiful.*

The Serenity Prayer
God, grant me the serenity to
Accept the things I cannot change;
Courage to change the things I can;
And wisdom to know the difference.
Living one day at a time;
Enjoying one moment at a time;
Accepting hardship as the pathway to peace.
Taking, as He did, this sinful world
As it is, not as I would have it.
Trusting that He will make all things
Right if I surrender to His Will;
That I may be reasonably happy in this life
and supremely happy with Him forever in the next.
Amen. [10]

CHAPTER 9

Developing and Nurturing Beautiful Relationships

PRINCIPLE 5

*A*while back, the media reported about a study that had been done on the value of girlfriends. The study found that women who have a lot of girlfriends actually live longer and healthier lives. We were thrilled. We figured we ought to live to be about 120! We love our girlfriends and value the relationships in our lives.

Relationships are a necessity in this world. We crave them. Why? Because we were created for them. Yet relationships can be one of the major contributors to emotional problems and stress when they include unresolved conflicts with people or dysfunctional attitudes.

And for many, it is a cyclical effect because they've never learned how to develop and nurture right relationships. The marriage didn't work. Not a shocker, neither did the one before that. The new friend didn't last long. No big surprise, neither did the last few. One of the greatest factors of failed relationships goes back to something we discussed in chapter 7: an attitude is like an undergarment—few people tell you when it is showing.

Had someone been honest with you or you with yourself, you might have realized that the marriage didn't work because forgiveness isn't a part of your life.

No relationship lasts without forgiveness as its cornerstone.

What about the friendships? They are a by-product of a "me" attitude. And no relationship lasts when the focus is centered on one person alone.

Relationships fail for a multitude of reasons. Sometimes it's because of no action on our part. But if we were honest, we would have to admit that sometimes relationships fail because of things "we" could change. And if you want to grow beautiful relationships, you'll have to begin by being honest with yourself.

As you grow beautiful relationships, you will also nurture such a level of honesty and trust that people will have no trouble telling you, "Uh, girlfriend, your slip is showing! And let me tell you, it isn't flattering on you. It cheapens your entire outfit."

 Karen says:

My mother had a saying. Well, she had a lot of sayings. But her favorite saying was "Actions speak louder than words." Her second favorite was "In order to have a friend, you must first be a friend." Those were the first words I heard whenever I came in griping about the way a friend had treated me, or complaining about an argument I had had with one of them. And it rings even truer today—especially in my work with women.

As a young adult, I was much more comfortable in a male environment. I often thought, *I would much rather work in an environment with fifty men than an environment that included two women!* Men don't seem to carry around baggage like women do. They aren't as critical or petty, and they are more apt to agree to disagree rather than spend needless energy "proving they were right."

On one occasion, at a very young age, I was given the opportunity to attend a board meeting with eleven men and two women and take notes for my boss who was on the board. In a matter of minutes, the meeting turned into a heated and intense disagreement that lasted three hours. Opinions were divided and tempers flared. After the meeting was over, the men were sitting at the table enjoying dinner while the two women were off by themselves, rehashing every detail of the meeting and fuming in the process. Then, their conversation digressed even further, moving away from the facts of the morning to personal attacks on the gentlemen whose opinions they disagreed with.

The following weeks were uncomfortable, and the women's attitudes, even toward me, were plain ugly. That entire experience never left me. It gave me new insights into the different ways men and women handle conflict. Now, I know nothing is ever exclusive to one gender or the other. I know there are some men who would have acted like the women in that meeting and some women would have acted like the men. But on the whole, women tend to hang on to conflict and carry it around as their own personal baggage. That is why, in order to truly have beautiful relationships, we each must realize the effort such relationships require and be willing to do whatever it takes to put aside our personal differences for the sake of those around us. As with all things truly beautiful, we must begin with ourselves. ❧

THE BEAUTY OF ME

There is a difference in thinking you're beautiful and knowing you're beautiful. People who think they're beautiful usually spend their life trying to convince you to think the same way. People who know they are beautiful don't have to prove anything to anyone. And those are the people who know how to make you feel beautiful as well. But there are also others, people who have never even realized they were truly beautiful.

So much of how we think of ourselves is connected to the relationships we have with others. And to live a truly beautiful life, it is imperative that we recognize what is right and what is wrong in our relationships. That's why it is important to evaluate those relationships. And our success, fulfillment, and happiness depend upon our ability to relate to the people in our lives effectively.

So in order to evaluate your relationships, begin by asking yourself, are my relationships mutually satisfying? Or are they only "others" focused? Am I abused verbally, emotionally, or even sexually in any of my relationships? Do my relationships build me up and energize me or do they drain me of my energy and joy? Do my relationships remain strong over the years or do they seem to fizzle out over time?

Your answers to these questions will help you determine the level of healthiness that you have in your relationships. Yet, someone once said that it is only possible to love and care for others as much as you love and care for yourself. And when you know that you're beautiful, you know that you deserve beautiful relationships.

A BEAUTIFUL RELATIONSHIP LIVES TO FORGIVE

A woman who truly desires to be *free to be beautiful* is a woman who forgives. Unfortunately, for many of us, this is one of our greatest areas of struggle. Yet nothing will ruin relationships more quickly than unforgiveness. A marriage can't last without it. A parent-child relationship will be miserable without it. A friendship will dissolve without it.

A forgiving spirit is a basic, necessary ingredient for beautiful relationships. We don't have to look much further than Princess Diana and Mother Teresa to see this. Princess Diana struggled to forgive, and she spent much of her life dealing with the pain of that unforgiveness. Mother Teresa didn't see forgiveness as something that was optional. She forgave all who hurt her, and she experienced peace as a result.

In the world in which we live, it's easy to feel wronged or slighted by those we have a relationship with. Sometimes it may be intentional. Other times it wasn't intended at all. And often the act of forgiveness is hard to find and even harder to offer. We might forgive, but we also want to add an extra dose of guilt. In return for our forgiveness, we expect to receive an added measure of grovel or vast and widespread vengeance.

Instead of bestowing our forgiveness, we pray something like this Irish prayer:

> *May those who love us, love us;*
> *And those who don't love us*
> *May God turn their hearts;*
> *And if He doesn't turn their hearts,*
> *May He turn their ankles,*
> *So we'll know them by their limping.*[11]

But forgiveness is really just another one of the actions that we take to change *us*. It frees us from our own guilt and removes the barriers that would hinder our relationships. And the ultimate effect is that we feel downright good about ourselves.

Often, however, you'll find that women who have trouble forgiving also have difficulty seeing their own faults and failures realistically. They are either terribly arrogant or tremendously insecure. People who keep score in relationships and find it more satisfying to carry a grudge than to set themselves free from their own baggage are people with, well, tremendous baggage. And that extra "mess" causes both emotional and physical side effects.

We were not created to be the judge. We were created to forgive. In order for you to be free, free to succeed, free to grow, free to discover, *free to be beautiful,* you have to realize you are free to forgive. It is a choice you make to set yourself free. And in order to have a lasting relationship, forgiveness won't just be a single occurrence of past transgressions, but a way of life—an everyday occurrence; a generous offering. And it's important that you be honest with yourself in the process because you may discover that the first person you have to forgive is yourself.

A BEAUTIFUL RELATIONSHIP LIVES TO GIVE

We are both blessed to live and work in an environment that's based on living by the Golden Rule: Do unto others as you would have them do unto you. The core of this directive is the discovery of the beauty that resides in each one of us. You can't live by this value until you first realize who you are and what you deserve. Once you realize that respect and unconditional love and forgiveness are available to you, then you realize they are a necessity for how you treat others.

Karen says:

Recently, I was shopping in a local department store. I was in a huge hurry and just needed to pick up a few things. The young woman who was waiting on me was obviously having a bad day. There were several other customers nearby that needed assistance as well, and yet this young lady was the only one available. I could tell she was taking no pleasure in this moment. She snapped at a woman who just asked a question and was grumpy with the lady who was in front of me in the line. When my turn came to be "helped," she wouldn't look at me or acknowledge me; she just kept working on her task. She obviously felt it necessary to complete it despite the fact that I was standing there.

When she finally gave me her attention, I smiled and said, "How are you today?"

She responded, "Too busy!"

I looked at her and said, "Well, you are obviously very good at what you do and your employer must think a lot of you." I had her totally confused at that point, but I did have her attention. I just continued. "The fact that you can handle all of this by yourself says a lot about your abilities, and they must really trust that you can get the job done by yourself."

She smiled and talked with me with seeming pleasure until she completed my purchase. As I left, I heard her address the next person in line much more pleasantly, and noticed that she was still smiling.

As I walked past the end of the line, the last person standing there said, "That is not what I would have said to her. She's not doing her job at all, and she doesn't deserve that compliment!"

Maybe she didn't "deserve" it, I thought. *But that compliment didn't cost me anything.*

A moment of encouragement can lift people out of the trapped and hopeless places in which they find themselves. It's amazing how the effects of giving can change people right before your eyes. When you treat people not as they are but as you want them to be and believe they can become, their perspective of themselves can change. Then it changes how they treat others. This girl's change in attitude might not have lasted long. In fact it might have faded as soon as the customer with the bad attitude checked out. But it helped my experience with her and the lady behind me. ᴒᴗ

Giving is freeing. And it is key in your relationship with others. It is putting yourself in someone else's place rather than putting him in his place. Treat people as if they are beautiful, and you're more than likely to enjoy beautiful people; people often respond in accordance with the way they are perceived.

Many times we think wonderful things about other people, yet they never know it. We tend to forget to praise and encourage, but have no problem remembering to criticize and complain. Praise is no good unless it is expressed. Whatever your position in a relationship, make it your responsibility to make others feel beautiful in the same way you have come to know that you are.

ᴒᴗ

Two common obstacles in our relationships often arise: criticism and conflict. Have you ever met them? If you've been in a friendship for any length of time, we're certain you have. Criticism often hides under the pretense of being "constructive." But we really don't believe there is any such thing. We prefer to give encouragement and honest feedback as opposed to "constructive criticism." We've discovered that words of support are far more effective than a critical analysis of someone's performance or actions. In fact, most of the time our criticism is only based on our personal opinion or our personal perception of reality.

What if, instead of trying to prove that our way is right and someone else's is wrong, we focused more on giving that person encouragement, direction, and feedback? A few kind words just might empower that person to discover for herself what the necessary course of action should be.

There are so many hurts that circumstances and the world inflict upon us, we need the constant reinforcement of encouragement.
~ BILLY GRAHAM

Words of encouragement change the atmosphere. Instead of one that is poisonous and avoided, it becomes a place of hope, courage, and confidence. Kind words dispel discouragement and bring out the best in people. Encouragement births life and releases potential that spurs accomplishment. So, be active in your encouraging of one another. Avoid criticizing or making critical comments. Be your friend's most enthusiastic cheerleader. Affirm your unconditional acceptance to those around you. And extend forgiveness regularly and quickly.

The frustrating thing about criticism is that it often arrives when we least expect it. And it rarely comes when we're on top, but instead, often shows up when we already feel like a failure. Criticism also seems to come at times when we least deserve it. Even when you've made an honest mistake or even a well-intentioned offering, some "dear soul" is bound to offer a bit of "encouragement" via the gift of criticism.

And worst of all is that criticism generally comes from people who are least qualified to give it. It's hard enough to hear criticism from a friend or a mate. But no one wants to hear it from a stranger—a person who has no personal relationship with you, no knowledge of your character, and certainly no vested interest in your success. Often it is those who know us least who offer the most criticism.

Criticism is rarely given in a helpful form. Sometimes it's accompanied by anger, jealousy, or envious rage. Criticism is seldom offered lovingly and graciously. More often than not, the words are delivered anonymously, like an unsigned bomb that appears harmlessly wrapped in a brown paper bag, but when opened, does unbelievable damage.

John C. Maxwell says that hurting people hurt people. And if you truly desire to develop and maintain strong and beautiful relationships, then an understanding of this concept is vital. We need to face our critics with grace and develop a little bit of grit along the way.

If you will see most criticisms as the petty moments that they are and choose to rise above them, then you will be the one that is free. Once you begin to focus solely on the issue rather than the person at the heart of the confrontation, you'll be better able to process the criticism for what it is and determine if it's something that you need to deal with or simply ignore.

CONFLICT

> *I have a great opportunity to do effective work here,*
> *although there are many people who oppose me.*
> ~ 1 CORINTHIANS 16:9 GWT

Criticism is one of the major contributors to conflict in relationships. Relationships and differences also go hand in hand. And when you are doing awesome things with your life, you can be sure that opposition will seek you out. But when you create an environment of mutual respect for those around you, conflict doesn't feel welcome for long. One of the most valuable ways to avoid conflict is to discover what precipitates it and learn how you deal with it in your own life.

Start by being honest with yourself. Answer the following questions:

- Do I run from conflict with others or do I face it and address it?

- In dealing with conflict, am I more likely to address the issue or the person?

- Am I quick to respond to another's need?

- Do I focus on and talk more about bad news or good news?

- Do I give people the benefit of the doubt or do I assume the worst?

If your relationships seem mired in conflict or criticism, start by changing your thought process. Think about the things that you appreciate about the people in your life. And then remind them of how much they mean to you. People tend to treat others according to how they see themselves, rather than how they really are. So by helping your loved ones find value within themselves, you'll also be helping yourself and building more beautiful relationships.

It's okay to love people and not like their behavior. It's even easier when you realize that the way we act toward others is a reflection of how we feel about ourselves.

We've each learned how to love this way and nurture our relationships because of the relationship we have with God. He loves us, even though He may not always approve of our words or actions, and when we ask Him, He promises to forgive us no matter what, freeing us to do the same. We desire to be like Him. And this affirmation is a daily reminder:

Through Me

Through me let there be kind words,

a warm smile, a caring heart.

Through me let there be a willingness

to listen and readiness to understand.

Through me let there be dependability,

steadfastness, trust and loyalty.

Through me let there be compassion,

forgiveness, mercy and love.

Through me let there be every quality

I find, O Lord in Thee.[12]

How we deal with others will determine how beautiful and fulfilled our relationships are. This is exemplified in the life of Mary Kay Ash.

Developing and Nurturing Beautiful Relationships

Everyone has a sign around their neck that says: "Make me feel special."
~ MARY KAY ASH

Mary Kay Ash was well known for the powerful effect she had through her words of encouragement. And this wasn't something she saved for large audiences or for her sales force at Mary Kay, Inc. She gave kind words to everyone around her, even those others never saw: the staff in hotel kitchens, the maids cleaning the guest rooms, the waiters waiting on the tables. For years, Mary Kay made it clear that God didn't create "a nobody," that everyone is "a somebody", and that everyone has something special and wonderful inside.[13]

Whenever Mary Kay attended an event at a hotel, she insisted on entering through the kitchen. There, she would greet the workers with a big smile that made them feel important. She often asked them how they were. When they would tell her they were fine, she would say, "No. You are great!" Each day, for as long as the event lasted, she'd go back to the kitchen, repeating her warm greetings. Hotel managers said she did more for their employees' morale and performance in those few moments than the managers had been able to do in years.

Many times, Mary Kay stood for hours greeting those who wanted to meet her or simply say something to her. She made each person feel as if he or she were the only person in the room, all the while giving no thought to her own comfort. Her kindness blessed others wherever she went. And this lesson is one that we can pass along by making others feel special even when it is not comfortable or convenient.

Bless—that's your job, to bless. You'll be a blessing and also get a blessing.
~ 1 PETER 3:9b THE MESSAGE

If that was really the heart of our relationships, we just might be surprised to watch how our words of blessing affect others, and in return affect us. Because life happens, there will be days when humans are just human. You won't be able to relate to them. You won't have any desire to work with them. You might not even want to hang around them. And that includes your friends, the people in your church or at the office, and even those under your own roof. But each one, when sifted through the funnel of blessing, will develop into the relationship you were uniquely crafted to celebrate.

Each relationship will be different. Your friends may be different from those you know at church; your family will be different from those you know at work. But each one has its unique place and special value. And each relationship will flourish under an attitude of blessing.

CHAPTER 10

Knowing the
Importance of Today

PRINCIPLE 6

 Karen says:

It has been said that 95 percent of what we worry about will never come to pass. Early in my career, a wise mentor suggested that in order to get the most out of today, I need to pay attention to two things: how I spend my time and what I worry about. She thought I should make a "worry box." So I did. It was similar to those little boxes that we made in school on Valentine's Day. And when any worry came to my mind, I would just write it down, place it inside the box, and move on. Then later I would designate a specific time to sit down in a nice, comfortable chair with a cup of coffee or tea, and "worry."

I had a plan. I would take an hour or so to pull each slip of paper out of the box and take time to worry. I was so good at it, I even decorated my box! I wanted to make it look better since I figured I would have it out on such a regular basis. But you know what I discovered? I found that when set aside, each one of my worries felt insignificant and virtually solved itself. This knowledge allowed me to realize something vital to a *beautiful* life: the importance of *today*. ᴧᴑ

My life has been full of terrible misfortunes most of which never happened.
~ MICHEL DE MONTAIGNE

*T*here is a distinct difference between planning for tomorrow and worrying about tomorrow. We could spend our entire life worrying about what might await us around the corner. But that prevents us from being effective today and offering something that could actually be of benefit to us tomorrow. Worry makes us forget that the only thing we truly can affect is what happens today.

Dr. Gillian Butler, a clinical psychologist at Oxford's Warneford Hospital says that worry is characterized by the question "What if . . ."

"It is about the risk or threat of something bad happening in the future and whether you could cope if it did. Whatever the causes, worriers will fret about anything and everything: finances, health, relationships and jobs—even when everything is going smoothly. This can lead to psychological symptoms such as fatigue, poor concentration, irritability and insomnia and physical symptoms such as palpitations, dry mouth, sweating, muscle tension, dizziness, faintness, indigestion, nausea, diarrhea, stomach ache and other aches and pains."

Did you have any idea worry could do all of that? Think of your life as if it were an hourglass. There are thousands of grains of sand in the top of the hourglass, and they all pass slowly and evenly through the narrow passage in the middle. Nothing you can do will make one grain of sand pass through more quickly or land any differently, without impairing the hourglass. Life is the same way.

We all pass through life, no matter what. Each morning shows up with a hundred things for us to do. We have a choice in how we handle our daily tasks. We can rush through our days in a kind of multi-tasking frenzy, hoping to manipulate the sand in our hourglass in order to accomplish as much as possible. Or we can allow each grain to fall evenly and steadily, as it should. And at the end of the day, it's amazing to find that we can accomplish just as much—maybe even more—when we're calm as when we're rushing around crazily. The added bonus is that nothing suffers in the process—not our mood, not our health, not our relationships.

There is wisdom in the words found in the middle of the Lord's Prayer, "Give us this day our daily bread." Notice it only asks for what you need for today. It doesn't complain about the stale bread you had yesterday. And it doesn't say, "Oh, God, what if something happens to prevent the trucks from delivering the bread to Wal-Mart?" It doesn't say, "What if I have to file bankruptcy and can't afford bread next week?" It just simply asks Him for what you need today.

What a novel concept—taking care of today. We aren't telling you not to plan. Everyone needs to prepare for the future. But in all of the preparing and saving and planning, it's easy to forget to live for today. And none of that is worth anything if we aren't even capable of enjoying it today.

Our main business isn't to see what lies dimly at a distance,
but to do what lies clearly at hand.
~ Thomas Carlyle

 Tina says:

A woman who had lost her husband was approaching bankruptcy and had fallen into a state of depression so severe that she was considering suicide. Thinking that maybe if she just got back to work, she would feel less hopeless, she called her old employer and asked for her job back. But the travel of the job and the dinners eaten alone only seemed to make her feel worse. To top it off, she was still barely able to make the car payment.

She was always afraid: afraid of not making the mortgage, afraid of not having enough to eat, afraid her health would fail her and she wouldn't be able to see a doctor. The only thing that kept her alive was the thought of her best girlfriend and young niece who would be heartbroken if she took her life. That, and the fact that she didn't even have enough money to pay for her funeral!

One day she was skimming through a book and came across the words, "Every day is a new life to those who will be wise enough to live it." She typed the phrase out on a piece of paper and made several copies to post around her house. She even emailed it to herself and wrote it on sticky notes that she pasted on her mirrors and in her car. She read those words everywhere she went, and each day she discovered something else worth living for.

Gradually, she began to let go of her fear. And each morning, she said aloud, "Today is a new beginning!" She still does it today. And if you met her, she'd tell you that she learned to let go of the past, not dwell on the future, and to live in the present. That's been a beautiful gift. ∿

Procrastination

Procrastination is my sin.
It brings me naught but sorrow.
I know that I should stop it.
In fact, I will—tomorrow.

A procrastinator puts off until *tomorrow* the things she has already put off today.

One of the greatest weapons against a beautiful life is procrastination. Mary Kay Ash said, "Most people live day to day, expecting that tomorrow they will do the things they wanted to do. They play a philosophy called a 'waiting game' or 'someday:' someday things won't be rushed, someday I'll be in a better position at work, someday the children will be in school. It's so easy to let tomorrow be your rule of life or to slip into the fatal error of living in retrospect or in the past or in prospects of the future, but *now* is the ever present time."[10]

If we were honest, we would admit that we all have a natural tendency to procrastinate and get sidetracked with unimportant things that seem very important at the moment. But once we learn some of the reasons we procrastinate and begin to recognize these things, we can begin to change our ways.

Here are a few we've come to recognize:

Lack of self-confidence. The fear of not being able to do something well can be enough to keep people from even starting in the first place. As you become more and more free in your personal journey, you'll begin to eliminate this kind of procrastination. As you become a woman who knows she has a job to do and are certain that you can do it, you'll find procrastination to be a thing of the past.

Insufficient Information. Many people stop doing something because they don't want to act until they know everything. After all, who wants to make a mistake? But life itself is a journey and many things are learned through trial and error. Be willing to make some mistakes, learning as you go. In doing so, you'll be less apt to put things off and more excited to try something new.

Poor problem-solving skills. Sometimes life seems to be nothing more than one crisis after another. Does it feel like you're either in the middle of a crisis, coming out of one, or going into one? Life happens and life can mean stress. It can be challenging to make good decisions and solve "problems" when you are stressed. The best way to deal with this is to carefully evaluate the problems in your life. Which circumstances are truly crises, and which ones are merely "bumps in the road?" A proper perspective on what is truly a problem will enable you to make the most of today.

Lack of planning. Planning is a major key to swift and decisive action. When we don't plan properly, we tend to flounder, and floundering usually leads to procrastination.

Ruts. You know what these are. Victims of chronic routine tend to freeze when faced with a decision that needs to be made or a task that is different from what they're used to. We can't be afraid of trying new things. In fact, the casual definition of "insanity" is doing the same thing day after day and expecting a different result.

Time wasters. These are those things that you do throughout the day that simply take up time, distracting you from what really needs to be done.

Attempting too much at once. Sometimes life seems to require superhuman powers, but even Wonder Woman knew when to hang up her lasso. You can't do it all, at least not all at once. And if you do, it's very possible that something will suffer in the process. Sometimes, trying to do too much becomes so overwhelming that we don't know where to begin and we end up doing nothing at all.

Unrealistic time estimates. Are you one of those people who says you'll be someplace at a certain time, but find that you're always running late? In order to focus on today, you must be realistic when you estimate how much time something will take. Don't be afraid to give everything the time it deserves.

Lack of specific priorities. Sometimes we start the day just running from one task to another. And at the end of the day, we find that we were so busy running, we didn't get anything done! Begin each day by mapping out a plan of attack. Decide what is priority and then go from there.

Failure to delegate. No one is great at everything. When we try to do everything ourselves, none of it gets done well. And, again, we find ourselves procrastinating because we're so overwhelmed and frustrated. So bring people around you who are gifted in certain areas and then trust them with that gift. Don't continue to try to do their job. Let them use their gifts and achieve what they were created to do.

Time really is a gift. It is laid out for us each morning, entrusting us with the treasure it holds. Every day, we are each credited with 86,000 seconds to fill. So we need to grab hold of every day and "seize it" with everything we have:

Seize the day by being *aware*. Aware of our opportunities. Aware of the invitation given us to live life as if it were an invitation to our own ball.

Seize the day by grabbing hold of the *opportunities* we've recognized. Don't let the ball go on without you. Get on the dance floor and dance, dance, dance!

Seize the day by taking quick *action* with *purpose*. Get your groove on because there are "moves" that only you can make. Remember on *Seinfeld* when Elaine showed her moves? No one else had moves like hers. She didn't wait until everyone else got on the floor. She "got the party started."

Seize the day by doing what *you are good at*. Can't dance? No big deal. You are great at something. So do that something and do it well. God places a dream in everyone's heart and He wouldn't do that without equipping you to accomplish it. Dig out whatever you've hidden in the back of your closet and wear it, girl!

Seize the day by doing the *daily's*. Karen calls this her "hour of power", and Tina calls it "Wakin' up at five to meet God on the sofa." Doing the "dailies" means that every day we set aside time to open our "gift" of today with the Giver of all gifts.

Knowing the Importance of Today

We are asked many times what this looks like. And it's different for both of us on any given day. But most days it just includes quiet time for spiritual and personal growth. And throughout the day, prayer time with our Maker, praying with the same openness and honesty that we would use if talking to our best girlfriend. Then we try to stop long enough to listen. You could read a book for growth, study a devotional, or listen to a lesson on CD that inspires you. You could even listen to inspirational music. But no matter what you do, set aside time for yourself.

So does today really matter? Well, think about this:

To know the value of one year,
ask the student who failed the final exam.

To know the value of one month,
ask the mother of a premature baby.

To know the value of one week,
ask the editor of a weekly news magazine.

To know the value of one day,
ask the wage earner who has six children.

To know the value of one hour,
ask the lovers who are waiting to meet.

To know the value of one minute,
ask the person who missed the plane.

To know the value of one second,
ask the person who survived the accident.

To know the value of one millisecond,
ask the Olympic silver medalist.

As you begin today to put aside the chains of procrastination, you'll begin to find new freedom in the beauty of this day:

Today I will be too calm to worry, too noble to get angry,
and too strong to be defeated!
Today, I believe that *anything* is possible...
I will walk through fear without hesitating.
Today I *will* take action.

 Tina says:

My daughter came to me as we were starting to write this chapter and asked me to coach her with the song she had to do for an audition for her school's play. After spending a couple of evenings rehearsing again and again, I quickly learned all the words right along with her:

> The sun'll come out tomorrow.
>
> Bet your bottom dollar that tomorrow,
>
> there'll be sun.
>
> Just thinkin' about tomorrow clears away the cobwebs
>
> and the sorrow, 'til there's none![14]

As I thought about those lyrics I wondered, *Where does that leave us today? What purpose does that offer us today? If the only thing we can hope for is the sun coming out tomorrow, does that mean we've given up on today?*

That isn't an option for us, ladies. Whatever happened yesterday—good or bad, failure or success—is gone forever. You can't go back. It's over. And whatever tomorrow might bring cannot be pulled into today, because it's simply not here yet.

But today? Today is a gift. And if you're breathing—you *are* breathing right? Well, if you are, the hope of possibility and opportunity is only found in today! What hope! ❧

Yesterday is history. Tomorrow is a mystery. And today?
Today is a gift. That's why we call it the present.
~ BABATUNDE OLATUNJI

CHAPTER 11

Planning Personal Growth
PRINCIPLE 7

*J*enni's mother called out to her at seven in the morning. "Jenni get up! It's time for school." There was no answer. She called again, only this time a bit louder. "Jenni, get up! It's time for school." Once more there was no answer. Exasperated, Mom went to Jenni's room and shook her daughter, saying, "Jenni, it's time to get ready for school."

"Mother, I'm not going to school today. There are fifteen hundred kids at school and every one of them hates me. I'm not going to school!"

"Get to school!" her mother replied abruptly.

"But Mother, all the teachers hate me, too. I saw three of them talking the other day and one of them was pointing his finger at me. I know they all hate me, so I am not going to school."

"Get to school!" her mother demanded again.

"But Mother, I don't understand it. Why would you want to put me through all of that torture and suffering?" Jenni protested.

"For two good reasons," Mom fired back. "First, you're forty-two years old. Second, you're the principal!"

Have you ever felt that way? Haven't we all! I'm sure most of us rejoiced at the thought of no more term papers or eight a.m. classes when we finally finished school. Maybe you miss the parties and the sorority socials, but you're probably relieved to be done with the "school" aspect of school. However, for many of us, when we left school, we also left behind structured and planned learning.

Today we learn by trial and error, by making a decision and then waiting to see whether it works or not. We trust "experience" to be the best teacher. But what if we made a decision that from now on, the learning in our life would be strategically planned?

If we were honest with ourselves, many of us would reveal that there are hopes and dreams that we buried years ago. And it's our desire that what you've read so far has made you realize that it's okay—in fact, it's vital to the legacy of your life—that those dreams no longer stay hidden. But that kind of growth doesn't automatically take place just because you live. Most of life's best and beautiful growth happens because you planned it that way.

Karen says:

I learned the lesson of personal growth backwards. There was a time when I had lost all direction in my life, feeling as if everything was falling apart and questioning if I even had a dream anymore. Then, I found some teaching tapes. Maybe just like you found this book. Now, being the kind of person who has to "feel" like I was doing something productive every day, I dug into those tapes and didn't stop until I had finished all one hundred lessons.

And after I was finished, I was surprised to find that new habits had begun to take shape in my daily routine. I realized that personal growth had developed from that time spent diligently studying and learning. The entire experience taught me something so valuable in regards to planned personal growth. And it created a desire to continue growing personally. I developed a daily practice of setting aside time for planned growth, and I still do it today. ᨇ

When you've done all you can do and given all that you have and you can't do anymore, your only option is to *become more.*

Tina says:

I want us to take a moment and look at a way of planning personal growth when you're gifted in a specific area. The best way I know to walk through this is by considering the steps I take in my singing.

The first thing is to ask yourself, *What would it take for me to tactically plan personal growth in this area?* Let's pretend that you're a singer and you've always dreamed of being a *star!* Your mama always told you that "No one sings as good as my baby." She reminds you every day that you need to get out there and show the world what you've got. You've been hesitant, but after watching a season of television talent shows you've gotten the bug.

So you're ready to sit down and lay out a plan that will develop your gift further and allow you to be the next "Idol." For example:

Get Real. Some of those people who sing on talent search shows sound really good, but then they're shocked when they're told they're not advancing to the next level. They thought they were fabulous! And they are certain the world is going to be in great peril because it has missed out on their "amazing" talent.

What happened? Well, for starters, the only person they might have asked is their mama. And mamas always think their babies are great. So don't just take your mother's word. You don't want to waste your time. Just because you sing in the shower doesn't mean it needs to be your profession.

Try this: Giving it your best effort, sing a three-minute song into a tape recorder. Listen to it and try to be as objective as possible. Attune your ear to the tone, the pitch, and your ability to stay within your vocal range.

Hire a coach. Take your tape to someone else—not your mama—for an honest opinion. Pay a professional vocal coach to give you an evaluation. Trust us, a professional will be honest and will help guide your talent. If you are serious about personal growth, you need an instructor. Why not? We hire trainers for everything else. If you can't afford one, there are enough books and DVDs in the market for almost any career choice imaginable.

Hang out with singers who are better than you. Don't just notice people you aspire to be, hang out with them! Ask what they are doing for personal growth in order to make their dream a reality. Notice their techniques and practices.

Don't know anyone personally? Then purchase the CDs of your favorite singers and study them. Read biographies of people who have achieved the dream you desire. And don't ever be intimidated by people who are better than you. Focus on what they are good at and apply it to your weak spots. Allow their gift to rub off on you.

Practice proper vocal skills. When you have been taught proper vocal skills, practice, practice, practice. Practice increases your consistency. Practice is proof of your commitment to steward your gift.

Focus on good health. Your vocal chords are flesh and blood so you must practice taking care of them. Drink water, get enough rest, avoid yelling or smoky clubs, and reduce stress.

Pablo Casals, the great cellist, was asked why, at eighty-five years old, he continued to practice five hours a day. He replied, "Because I think I'm getting better." Whether you're a writer, a teacher, a mother, a sales representative, or an executive, you need to be diligent in becoming even better at what you do.

Personal growth takes time. It sometimes requires financial investment. It will mean change. But it will make all the difference in what you want to do and who you want to become on your journey toward freedom. ᴧ

SETTING OUT A PLAN

When you begin to make a real plan for personal growth, you will have to carve out time to implement the plan in your life. And the best time to start is today. Carve out thirty minutes and begin giving it your best. You might be surprised to find out that just like physical exercise, once you start seeing results, it will be even easier to do it the next time.

Most personal growth plans reach their maximum potential when we include all three areas of our life: our *spiritual growth*, our *professional growth*, and our *physical growth*. There may be other areas that need attention in your life in order to reach your potential, but most of life falls into these three categories.

Plan your time according to what fits best in your lifestyle.

We all lead different lives. Some of us spend most of our time at home, others are in their cars, and others are in the office. So it is important that you determine what time of the day best works for you and then manage your life to make sure that you leave that time for yourself.

Remember that you probably won't be able to work on every area of your life in only thirty minutes. Your spiritual growth might be at one point in your day, perhaps first thing in the morning. Your physical growth might have to take place at another time, after work or over your lunch hour for example. And you'll need to focus on professional growth at still another time.

Plan a system that works for you.

Karen's personal growth plan looks like this:

- Read and study two books a month.

- Listen to seven audio lessons every week.

- Write down thoughts and ideas from each lesson.

- Note and plan application of what I am learning.

- List ways I was effective because of the books or lessons each day.

- Attend one conference or workshop a quarter.

- List daily blessings.

Try to find books and CDs that target the specific areas in your life that you are working on. Take advantage of unused segments of time. For example, you might not have time to read a book in a week, but if you spend a lot of time driving, you can listen to audio lessons in the car. Don't be afraid to skim through books or set aside CD's that aren't meeting your expectations. In some instances, it's okay to not finish what you start. If the material is not helpful, don't spend your energy trying to finish it just for the sake of completing a lesson. Move on to other material that is more geared to the areas of your life you are focusing on at that time.

After you begin to implement your own personal system for growth, you'll find that you are more aware of opportunities for learning. As you devote time each day to move toward your potential, you will find that with each step, you are growing more and more *free to be beautiful.*

GETTING STARTED

Now that you've made your plan and set aside time to implement your plan, it's time to get started.

Every plan needs accountability. Find someone, a friend or mentor who can give you direction, support, and feedback as you begin your journey. Talk with this person about your goals and what you hope to accomplish, and ask her (or him) to help keep you focused and encouraged in your task.

Make the most of your personal time. This is the time that we talked about in the last section, time you've set aside specifically for personal growth. Use the time to reflect, plan, evaluate, and review your strengths and your weaknesses. Study material that specifically speaks to your strengths, style, and goals.

Take time to focus on your own spiritual development. Feed your faith daily so you can respond to life's challenges rather than simply reacting. Spiritual growth has a way of seeping into all other areas of life, promoting growth and beauty as it develops.

An effective plan also needs a fitness plan. The way you feel affects the way you perform and produce. It also reflects your self-image.

As you get started, make a real effort to be *aggressive* and *intentional* in your efforts toward personal growth. Reaching out for your potential frees you to live life to the fullest, and nothing could be more beautiful.

TEACH THE THINGS YOU'VE LEARNED

Have you ever been a tutor? Every day you should try to apply the things that you are learning. Nothing challenges you more than sharing those things with someone else. This will motivate you to study more and work harder, and then you get the joy in watching someone else discover the things that you have already learned.

❧

To truly be *free to be beautiful*, personal growth is essential—especially for those of you who even today feel as if you are trapped in a stagnant job or position, or those who are in a relationship that isn't healthy, or those who truly desire a life that's filled with hope and potential. You need a breakthrough to go to the next level. Don't just sit back and wait for the next "experience." Instead, it's time to take life and strategically make it an experience. Remember, true change is never quick and rarely easy. Growth is a process. The results may not show immediately, but you can be assured that underneath the surface, change is taking place.

Think about planting tulip bulbs in September. It's hard work. You have to dig a hole for each one individually and make sure the bulb is completely covered. Then, when you go outside the next day, all you can see is dirt. And for the next five or six months, you'll still only be able to see dirt. But the truth is, something is happening under the dirt. Just because you can't see it doesn't mean it isn't occurring. By March, a little green sprout will begin to break through the dirt. And by April the entire garden will be filled with the most beautiful flowers you've ever seen.

The same is true with your life. You are creating something beautiful. So keep sowing. Keep watering. And know that every day you are growing—growing one step closer to being *free to be beautiful.*

To be what we are, and to become what
we are capable of becoming
is the only end of life.
~ ROBERT LOUIS STEVENSON

CHAPTER 12

Discovering the
Beauty of Change
PRINCIPLE 8

 Tina says:

Do you know what sunshine on a cloudy day feels like? To me it comes wrapped in homemade chocolate chip cookies, loaded with semi-sweet chocolate chips. It's a singing-in-the-rain and it-is-well-with-my-soul kind of feeling.

But one New Year's Eve, as I looked ahead to the next year, I knew that my New Year's resolution that year was going to have to involve my health. I had to make a change, a personal decision that my food choices were going to be different than they had been in the past.

However, as far as my calendar was concerned, it was still December 31, and this girl still had one more night of chocolate chip cookies left in her. So I made a batch and enjoyed every aroma, every texture, and every taste of those cookies. Besides, I wasn't planning on eating the *entire* batch! I enjoyed every bite of my two cookies and wrapped the remainder to freeze for the future.

That evening, as I was putting the cookies away, my husband asked me to leave out two for him to eat before bed. Then my son came and pulled out two more for a bedtime snack. So, there those four cookies sat. Four lonely cookies, placed in a Ziploc bag on the counter.

January 1 arrived. Pouring myself a fresh cup of Starbucks, I noticed the cookies sitting abandoned on the counter. Those guys had forsaken their cookies! I would have never treated them in such a way. I would have eaten every crumb of those delicious cookies had I saved them for *my* bedtime snack.

I bet you're thinking right about now that I sat down and enjoyed those cookies with my Starbucks coffee that morning. Not on your life. They weren't mine to eat and besides, you forgot, it was Monday, the first day of my new commitment. No ma'am, I didn't eat those cookies until Tuesday night around nine o'clock. What happened, you ask? What happened to the commitment? What happened to making a personal change? Well, in the words of Mae West, "I used to be Snow White . . . but I drifted."

In a society of fast-food restaurants and lose-weight-fast promises all located within blocks of each other, the simple fact still remains: just because you have a dream doesn't mean your circumstances will change. But *because* you have a dream, you *can* change your response to your circumstances. So how do we do this, you ask?

My decision to go on a diet and to make better food choices in the coming year all began with a thought. But the outcome was determined by my behavior, which motivated my feelings. ⌇

EVERY CHALLENGE TO CHANGE STARTS WITH YOUR FEELINGS

*S*o you ask, if you can control your thoughts and know that your feelings come from thoughts, can you control your feelings by controlling your thoughts? Absolutely. Few people control their thinking. This is the reason many people fail to govern their lives.

Ever been full of stinkin' thinkin'? If so, it's time to take a bath in personal growth. What you believe and what you think about is crucial to discovering the beauty of change. Because inevitably, what you believe about yourself is the truth that you will live.

Dr. Phil, the well-known television talk-show host, told a story once about one of his son's birthday parties. He handed out helium-filled balloons and one of the children asked him, "If I let go of my balloon, will it go up real high?" Dr. Phil responded, "Sure it will, son. It's what's inside your balloon that makes it go up real high."

The same is true for us. The depth of what is inside us will determine the heights that we will reach. And in order to discover the beauty of change, we must pay attention to the things that we dwell on.

> When you change your *thinking* you change your *beliefs*.
> When you change your *beliefs* you change your *expectations*.
> When you change your *expectations* you change your *attitude*.
> When you change your *attitude* you change your *behavior*.
> When you change your *behavior* you change your *performance*.
> When you change your *performance* you change your *life*. [15]

No one can determine your need for change but you. It is a personal choice that creates widespread effect. But the only way change will last is when it is done because you realize you can no longer live without it. Once you determine that you need to change, you must be assured that it is possible. Just look around you. The evidence of change's possibility is everywhere.

It's evident in the life of the alcoholic who determines to make a change and regains his family. It is evident in the life of the teenage runaway who decides to return home and is now in college creating a destiny. The impact of change is all around you. And the effects of change reach far beyond the single person who makes the personal decision.

If you really wanted to be any different, you would be in
the process of changing right now.
~ FRED SMITH

Friends, we simply can't improve unless we are willing to change. And we can't change until we realize that beliefs control everything we do. If you believe you *can* change, then you are right. If you believe you *cannot* change, you are also right. What we expect is generally what we accomplish. And as we revealed in the beginning of this chapter, what we become outwardly is really only a reflection of what we believe inwardly.

Have you ever noticed that when we bring our babies home from the hospital, the first thing we do is buckle them up? As they grow, the continued practice of our buckling them up creates a habit that eventually transfers to them buckling themselves up. Now every time they get in the car, the first thing they do is hook their seat belts. They learned it wasn't an option. Now it has become a way of life. The habit has formed them.

Change is a good thing when it brings growth. And change will bring growth if we approach it with the right attitude. When you have a "beautiful" attitude, all change—whether positive or negative—will be a learning experience, which can result in a growing experience. But simply "doing" will never create growth. In fact, the old saying "practice makes perfect" isn't necessarily true either. Practice does make permanent, but it's only when we are practicing the right things that we will experience growth.

Every moment of change begins by asking yourself: *Do I even have the desire to change? Do I really want to change?* Nothing will determine the success of change more than your desire to do it. When everything else has failed, desire alone can keep you focused on the areas of your life that need to be reconstructed or realigned. When you truly desire change, you can overcome nearly every obstacle, and in the end, find true freedom. When you realize that change is possible, you'll gain confidence and hope because you know that there is the possibility of even greater growth in the future.

But what if I slip back into those old habits? What if I eat the cookies left on the counter? Does that mean I can't ever try again? If we've learned anything, we've learned that being *free to be beautiful* is a daily journey. It's reminding ourselves every day that we are more than capable of doing today what we failed to accomplish yesterday. And the doubts that we had yesterday are the doubts that we simply have to fight harder today.

Change is a process. And we will make mistakes. Some people make mistakes by waiting for God to change their circumstances. Others wait for their circumstances to change their behavior. Both lead to allowing our feelings to motivate our behavior instead of our behavior motivating our feelings. To avoid this trap, try to simply focus on the daily aspects of living as you embrace change in your life.

Consider these ideas that have proven to be beneficial for our own lives:

Take one day at a time. Anyone can face the battle of today, but when we add on yesterday's battle, and then tack on what we're worried about tomorrow, life seems to be nothing but confusion. Yesterday's mistakes can lead to tomorrow's victories if we simply remain steadfast in focusing on today. Live one day at a time—*today!*

Develop good habits. Any habit starts with our thoughts. The process for developing habits, good or bad, is the same. Make a daily commitment to the change you are trying to implement in your life. Habits are not instincts; they are acquired actions or reactions. They don't just happen; they are caused.

 Karen says:

Six years ago I made a decision to change my lifestyle. I had been taking my health for granted for quite a while. I wasn't doing what I knew I needed to be doing in terms of my health. My motto was "eat when you're old and sleep when you're dead." How's that for a way of living?

Now, I love junk food. I mean I *really* love junk food. And so almost every day I would grab whatever was the "junk food of choice" that day. I knew it was bad for me, but, well, it was just plain good. I also loved my work and was known to spend many a night or middle of the night, happily working away while everyone else was asleep.

I have always been blessed with the ability to function with very little sleep. But as we all know, the body requires sleep in order to operate at its most productive level.

Since my family's history is scary regarding longevity, I realized that I needed to make some *big* changes in how I approached my way of life. I decided I was going to get fit, eat better, and sleep!

In high school I had been rather athletic. I ran track, was a cheerleader, and even enjoyed golf in those years before I had children. But for the last sixteen years, the only exercise I got was walking from my bedroom to my office, which was all under the same roof. So, the first day of my new exercise program, I didn't show up. I didn't make it on day two either due to the rain. On day three, I believe we had sun, but, my word, it was cold out there. And when I did finally show up, which was nothing more than exiting my house and walking around my neighborhood, I was so inconsistent, a burglar wouldn't have been able to stage a crime around me that's for sure.

So, I decided I needed a treadmill. That way, all of my excuses would be removed. It worked! People even began to notice the change in me. And I began to enjoy the results myself. Then, when I realized one Coke cost me a mile on the treadmill, even that didn't seem as enjoyable.

Six years later, I still battle the excuses, but the habits I have developed have served me well. I decided to take it to another level, and I hired a personal trainer. He pushes me, doesn't let me off the hook, and keeps things changing so I don't get bored. I remember hearing one time that you can get to a place where you miss the workouts if you don't keep doing them. I thought someone would have to be crazy to feel that way about exercise. But guess what. I do miss them! And I've learned that habits become a way of life.

Some things I do much better than others. I still have trouble in the food and sleep areas every now and then. Even worse, I smoke cigarettes and I hate it. But my goals are to continue to motivate myself to let go of that bad habit. And so it goes. ৬

As we both have gone through the daily task of implementing change in our own lives, we have been fortunate to find some things that really helped along the way. One of them is finding a friend to hold us accountable. Everything seems easier when someone shares your same goals, supports you as you reach toward those goals, and reminds you to hold onto your dreams on those days when you might forget. Surround yourself with people who are helping you in making your beautiful changes.

Another big help in implementing change in our life can be found in role models. Remember when Jennifer Anniston's hairstyle, "the Rachel," was the in thing? Every schoolgirl ran to the beauty shop to look like her. People can have that same effect on us as well. So find a person who you greatly respect and admire; then use that person as a model for your own life. Learn how he or she responds and why. Use this person as your guide for developing healthy self-esteem and confidence.

And don't be afraid to take an honest account of the mistakes you've made—the mistakes that have precipitated your desire to make changes in your way of life. By recognizing them, you'll be better able to avoid these same mistakes in the future.

Then whatever you do, reward yourself! Even small victories feel better with a reward. Maybe it's a night at the movies with your girl-friends. Maybe it's a pedicure. Maybe it's just an afternoon without the kids and a good book. Take time to recognize that even small achievements are achievements. And once again, the net result of three steps forward and two steps back is still one step toward freedom!

The only thing that stands between a man and what he wants from life is often merely the will to try it and the faith to believe that it is possible.
~ RICHARD M. DeVOS

Discovering the Beauty of Change

There will be days you'll want to give up. To be honest, there may even be weeks. But the results of a daily resolve to things that will make you truly beautiful can be motivation enough for the next challenge of change that you choose to confront. And don't get anxious, because you may not see immediate change. Be patient. You will see that even your circumstances might change when you are diligent in maintaining an attitude of confidence in your commitment.

We must become the change we want to see.
~ MAHATMA GANDHI

Summing it all up, friends, I'd say you'll do best by filling your
minds and meditating on things true, noble, reputable, authentic,
compelling, gracious-the best, not the worst; the beautiful,
not the ugly; things to praise, not things to curse.
~ PHILIPPIANS 4:8 THE MESSAGE

So, if all change begins with our thoughts, then we would say, "Yes, that sums it up."

CHAPTER 13

Making Beautiful Choices
PRINCIPLE 9

To improve any area of your life, you must make beautiful choices. The choices you make by accident are just as significant as the choices you make by design.

An elderly carpenter was ready to retire. He told his employer of his plans to leave the house building business and live a more leisurely life with his wife, enjoying his extended family. He would miss the paycheck, but he needed to retire. He and his wife could get by.

The contractor was sorry to see his good worker go and asked if he would build just one more house as a personal favor. The carpenter said he would. But in time, it was easy to see that his heart was not in his work. He resorted to shoddy workmanship and used inferior materials. It was an unfortunate way to end his career.

When the carpenter finished his work and the builder came
to inspect the house, he handed the front door key to the carpenter.
"This is your house," he said. "My gift to you."

What a shock! What a shame! If the carpenter had only known
he was building his own house, he would have done it all so differently.
Now he had to live in the home he had built none too well.

Who we are today is the result of the choices we made yesterday.
And so it goes that tomorrow we will become what we choose today.
Unfortunately, the decisions that we make on a daily basis are often
done in a distracted way. We are distracted by our pending responsibilities or our desire to be somewhere else. And often in the middle
of what we've been called to do today, we give less than our best effort,
just like the carpenter. Then, when handed the keys to what we have
created, we realize we are required to live in what we have built. Had
we known that in advance, we would have done things differently.

Take a moment and think of yourself as the carpenter. Think
about your own personal house. Each day you hammer a nail, place
a board, or erect a wall. Build wisely. It is the only life you will ever
build. Even if you only possess it for one more day, that day deserves
to be lived graciously, purposefully, and with dignity.

Your life today is the result of your choices in the past.

**Your life tomorrow will be the result of the choices you
make today. Choose poorly and you build a shoddy life.**

Choose wisely and you build a beautiful life.

Either way, it is your choice.

Making Beautiful Choices

We all have those moments we wish we could undo: the foot-in-the-mouth hurtful words, the forgotten thank-you, the uninformed decision, the stolen moment of youth. And the results of those poor decisions brought hurt feelings, wrong perceptions, and possibly detrimental results to our families, our colleagues, or ourselves.

But in life it is never too late to right wrongs. Most people can discern motive. And when you've made an unintentional mistake, often a heart-felt apology or thank-you can repair the damage and change the wrong into something beautiful.

You will also be amazed to find that as you begin to make right choices, those things that used to feel muddled or unclear in your life now begin to gain clarity. Never underestimate the value of small, positive choices. Every small choice eventually meets with the next and creates a beautiful life. And there is nothing more beautiful than a person who is continually making choices in life that reflect a fruitful, confident, and joyful individual.

As you watch the effects of the positive choices you are making in your life, you'll be motivated to make even more! You'll be excited to focus on what comes next. Then, with each beautiful choice, you will create in yourself a desire to meet every day with renewed energy and life.

Then when life comes, as it always does, the difficult times won't seem quite as tough because of your proven track record. Once you have established in yourself that you are capable of not only making, but also living right choices, you will gain the confidence to face the difficulties life will offer.

When you increase the percentage of choices you make intentionally, you decrease the number of lessons you learn accidentally.
~ JOHN C. MAXWELL

Each day—dare we say, every moment—we are making choices whether consciously or unconsciously. And each choice will have an inevitable result. Some of your choices will create an atmosphere of encouragement and a desire to work harder and become better—in effect, to "build up."

Other choices you make create an atmosphere of discouragement and frustration—one that "tears down." And some choices will do nothing more than cause you to remain exactly where you are.

Certain factors usually determine which kind of atmosphere we are more likely to create. Sometimes the attitudes and choices we saw in the homes we grew up in are reflected in our decision-making today. Friends also play a key role when it comes to influencing choices. Often, our decisions are simply the result of the way we are wired or perhaps a reaction to past successes and failures. And for many of us, the choices that we make reflect the way we feel about ourselves.

Each of these factors in your life can easily direct your current path. But no factor *has* to determine the direction of your future. In determining where you need to be, it is helpful to know which personality type you tend to gravitate toward. Then you can begin to create a life of choices that will move you closer to the freedom of living a beautiful life. Let's take a look at three types of choices and the personality types associated with each one:

CHOICES THAT BUILD US UP

People in this group are likely to think of themselves as "works in progress." The choices that they make are often small, but always intentional. Each choice moves them forward, whether for the day or for their future. People in this group are also aware that the choices they make will affect their self-image and how they view their worth.

They make choices that are proactive rather than offensive or defensive.

People in this group also have a heightened awareness of the responsibility for their choices and their actions. They know that an imperfect world requires determined living rather than a "go with the flow" mentality. It just isn't an option for them.

CHOICES THAT TEAR US DOWN

People in this group tend to be a reflection of their past failures. And as we've learned, that perception does nothing but make them their own worst enemy. They also operate by flying off the handle and taking unmeasured chances rather than seeing opportunities and being strategic in how they handle them. They see life through the lens of what can go wrong instead of all that could turn out right. And when looking out the window, they're far more likely to see the darkness than the daylight that is only moments away.

CHOICES THAT CAUSE US TO REMAIN THE SAME

People in this group are far more focused on short-term satisfaction than long-term results. They often go for the "quick fix," the temporary solution, the "just enough" mentality. They don't want to experience uncomfortable situations so they avoid them altogether, even if those situations would produce the greatest results. They are comfortable just being invited to the party; they're not too interested in being the hostess.

The beautiful thing about choices is that no matter what kind of choices we've made in the past, we don't have to stay there. It is possible to become beautiful people who make beautiful choices. And those choices will not only benefit our own life but the lives of those around us.

At the end of the day, choices rest on our shoulders and on our shoulders alone. Don't be afraid to learn. Learn from people who can teach you something about good decision-making. Read books that can challenge you to be intentional in your choices. And don't be afraid to practice what you've discovered. Don't be afraid to take that first step. Even if it's a small one, it will only create an attitude of success that will eventually lead to bigger steps. Don't be ashamed or afraid to think big. Live with a determined attitude toward life, and you'll be amazed at what you'll accomplish.

Making good choices can be a daunting task: the glazed Krispy Kreme or the chocolate one, a cold glass of milk or bottled water, one or a dozen. Some choices in life will offer you the pleasure of the experience. Others will simply make you sick.

Your life is the sum result of all the choices you make, both consciously and unconsciously. If you can control the process of choosing, you can take control of all aspects of your life. You can find the freedom that comes from being in charge of yourself.

You can:

Choose to love—rather than hate.

Choose to smile—rather than frown.

Choose to build—rather than destroy.

Choose to persevere—rather than quit.

Choose to praise—rather than gossip.

Choose to heal—rather than wound.

Choose to give—rather than grasp.

Choose to act—rather than delay.

Making Beautiful Choices

Choose to pray—rather than despair.

Choose to forgive—rather than curse.

Each day brings a new opportunity to choose.[16]

CHAPTER 14

Giving Abundantly
PRINCIPLE 10

*E*ver heard the story of Hattie? Hattie was a young girl from Philadelphia. A neighborhood minister started a Sunday school program for children in her community and she was at the very first meeting. The room they had chosen for that first meeting was small, so they had to turn a few of the children away. When Hattie got home that night and laid down to go to sleep, her heart was sad because some of her friends had been turned away and had not heard the message.

Two years later, Hattie died. Her mom and dad sent for the pastor. When he arrived they gave him an old red purse they had found under Hattie's pillow. It had fifty-seven pennies inside. She had earned every one of them by running errands. And with the pennies was a handwritten note that read, "This is to build the church bigger so more children can go to Sunday school."

The minister carried Hattie's purse with him to the pulpit the next Sunday after Hattie's funeral. He took each of the fifty-seven pennies and dropped them one by one back into the worn red purse so that all of the congregation could see. He told them that Hattie had given all that she had. Few dry eyes could be found in the room.

After the service, a man who had been visiting approached the pastor. "Pastor, I'll sell the church some land that I have for fifty-seven pennies," he said. But this wasn't just any piece of land. This was a coveted piece of property that would be perfect for a new church building.

Before long, every news outlet caught wind of Hattie's story and money began to come from everywhere. Today, Temple Baptist Church is one of the most impressive facilities in Philadelphia. At the turn of the 1900s, it seated thirty-three hundred people. And it all began with the generous heart of a little girl named Hattie.

> I am only one, but I am one.
>
> I cannot do everything, but I can do something.
>
> And what I can do, I ought to do.
>
> And what I ought to do, by the grace of God, I will do.
>
> I will make a difference.[17]

Ask anyone who does it, and they'll tell you: Giving increases living. Why? Because of all the things that we do in life, giving is the one thing that takes our eyes off of us. Do you remember how you felt in those days after September 11, when the United States was focused on something bigger than our small lot in our own neighborhood? Many were moved to help, even though they didn't know the victims' names or the names of their children. It was a feeling of generosity and unity that we very rarely feel in such a corporate way. But it is a feeling that is available to us every day.

Why wait for a disaster to be generous? Why not, like any other aspect of your life, focus strategically on making giving a part of planned growth? Could it be that easy? We believe it can be. We believe a lifestyle of giving can be developed like any other "beautiful" attribute you are trying to achieve. Just as you can determine to create a beautiful attitude, you can also determine to create a spirit of giving.

Now don't make the initial mistake of thinking that you have to be wealthy to be generous. Generosity isn't based on how much money you have in your bank account. It is about the resources you have in your life. Some of the most generous people in the world will never be found on the Fortune 500 list. In fact, they won't even be found on their local bank's 500,000 list. And in much the same way, some of the wealthiest people in today's world are also some of the least generous.

Generosity is not about money; it's about an attitude of the heart. In order to be *free to be beautiful,* you must also be free to give. And the desire to give is the only resource you need.

 Karen says:

My mother used to always say, "There's greater joy in giving than receiving." Now, as a kid, I wasn't quite sure that her information was correct. I mean, there wasn't much I loved more than getting presents. And at that age, I didn't have a lot of experience in giving much of anything. But as with all things our mothers tell us, there was that moment when I finally *got* what she was trying to teach me.

When I was about five years old, my mother was going to visit a family that had recently moved to our neighborhood. She asked me to come along. While they were visiting, I tried to occupy myself and let them talk their grown-up talk. But their conversation sounded rather interesting so I leaned in to hear every word.

I'll never forget hearing our new neighbor tell my mother that once she gave her children their lunch money, she didn't have any money left to have lunch herself. Until that moment, it had never occurred to me that someone wouldn't be able to have lunch. I guess I had not given much thought to where my lunch came from since it was always there.

Even at five years old, I was overwhelmed with the feeling that we needed to do something to help this family. It was so strong I tried to make my mother leave the house at once. I knew there was money in my room and I wanted to give it to the lady, now! My mother finally got the message and took me home. I got the little bit that I had saved and went back down the street and handed it to my neighbor for her next lunch. I'll never forget the feeling that giving my money away gave to me. Complete satisfaction.

I know that my few pennies didn't solve her problem. They probably didn't even buy a complete lunch. But they allowed me to see what giving could do in my own life. And that experience is still one of my most vivid memories from my childhood, all because of the joy I felt in that moment. ❧

Today's society is all about *me*. It's all about wearing the right dress so *I* can make the right impression, participating in the right clubs or social events so I can feel good about myself, driving the right car so I can make the right statement. It's pretty easy to focus on nothing but *me*. Yet we forget that no matter how big our own situation may seem at this moment, there is someone else who has a bigger problem, a tougher road, a more heartbreaking situation than our own. And did you also know that you could be the very instrument used to make the situation in someone else's life different—dare we say, better?

You were created for a reason greater than yourself. If you miss this one truth you will never know what it is to be *free to be beautiful*. Yet maybe you feel that you have nothing to give. Oh, but you do. You have a smile, a compliment, a hug, a touch. You know how those make you feel. They are contagious. And you can't outgive your capacity. You will always have the capacity to give more. As you give, you will be amazed that not only are your own needs being met, they are often met exceedingly, abundantly, and beyond your expectations.

Alison's husband had just returned home to recuperate after a hospital stay when her friend Michelle came by and took her laundry—five kids' worth of laundry. She returned a few days later with every piece, clean and neatly folded. Did Michelle just have a bunch of extra time on her hands and needed something else to do? Do any of us? No, she saw an opportunity to give. It took her time, of which nothing is more valuable. That is what made her gift even more priceless to her friend.

Giving frees us. But ultimately it is about more than a moment; it is about creating a lifestyle—a lifestyle of generosity that we must choose to walk every minute of every day of every year until our life is over.

But what if I fall back into my old ways? We all have those moments. We all ask, "What's in it for me?" from time to time.

We are called to be self-effacing, self-forgetting, self-sacrificing, and selfless. We aren't called to be self-absorbed, self-indulgent, self-involved, and self-seeking. So it's time that we take some practical steps to making giving a daily part of our lives:

Say thank you or write a personal note to acknowledge something someone has done for you.

Give a pat on the back, a smile, a hug, or a phone call to say hello.

Bake a cake or pick a flower.

Buy chocolate-covered cherries if you know that it is her favorite.

Take Baley, your girlfriend's "Starbucks-loving" sheepdog, a vanilla Crème Frappuccino just because you love her. Now that's generous!

 Tina says:

I've been known to have a good pity-party or two in the past. They even feel good in that moment. Karen actually has a "Tantrum Mat." It consists of a piece of paper with two feet drawn on it. On occasion, when she needs a "moment", she'll hide where no one can see her, take her mat, and let loose! She throws herself a good one. Then she puts the mat away and goes on about her day.

But because both of us truly aspire to live *free to be beautiful,* we have learned that those can only be moments of our lives, not lifestyles. And trust me, we've had our share of things that could keep us there. I know what it's like to be stolen from and feel the sting of being violated. To watch as what took our whole life to achieve is taken away. But we can't remain there.

Please don't think we've mastered this. This is something we have to determine to do daily. But we also see now how even small ways of giving affect people's lives.

My sweet sister-in-law Kathy recently had eighty helium balloons sent to her dad for his eightieth birthday. He called her to say the roof was coming off the house. But he loved it!

One of my husband's employees sends a Christmas gift each year and addresses the card to both Mike and Tina. She doesn't work for me and wouldn't have to acknowledge me at all, yet she does. I'm not sure if she's ever fully realized how much it means to me that she includes me. She's known for having a giving heart, and it's not about the gifts she gives. But . . . thanks for the steaks, Janet!

Early in our marriage, Mike and I owned a pizza restaurant. We were working long and hard every day and still operated in the red most months. One particular month we didn't even have enough money to make our mortgage payment. We had used our credit card once before to make a payment and thought we might have to do it again.

I remember getting tired and frustrated. I let God know: *God, do you see our need? Do you hear our prayer? We've given. We've worked. We've waited. We've tithed.* We knew we had done all we could do. We had been faithful to the principles we had been called to live by, and now we would wait and see how God would provide.

Late one night we were coming home from the restaurant and stopped to pick up the mail. There was a check for five hundred dollars from my aunt and uncle. They were living in Saudi Arabia at the time for my uncle's job. They had been praying and felt impressed to send a gift to us—a five-hundred-dollar gift that was more than enough to cover our mortgage.

This was a defining moment for us—especially when we realized that the check had been in the mail for over two weeks. It was on its way even before we realized the depth of our own need. It really doesn't matter how God does it, whether He blesses you with a second job or allows you to sell something of your own to make up your need, but He will be faithful to provide when you are faithful to give. ❧

But good people will be generous to others
and will be blessed for all they do.
~ Isaiah 32:8 NLT

 Karen says:

Do you remember the story I shared with you in the beginning of
this chapter about giving my neighbor my saved money when she
couldn't afford lunch? Well let me add this. The friendship between our
families grew to be a strong relationship over our years living near one
another. The father of that family was assigned overseas for three years,
which made it seem as if a single mother was leading this family. Our
family decided we would share my father with her and her three girls.

He taught our neighbor how to drive and then helped her find
a car. When something around their house needed a man's touch,
my father always lent a hand. We shared many meals together, and
they even came with us on a family vacation one year. Eventually we
moved away and gradually lost regular contact with the family. But
over the years, we always caught up on the "big" events: marriages,
births, etc. After a couple more moves, however, we lost contact
completely.

Ten years later, we moved back but didn't really reconnect with
this family. And shortly after our return, my father became ill with
his heart. The supervising nurse at the hospital recognized my father's

name on the surgery schedule. Come to find out, she was the youngest daughter of that family. She immediately took our family under her "professional wing." My father received her best care, her special treatment. Then when visitors were finally allowed, her mother and sisters were some of the first to arrive. It seemed like old times.

After my father was released from the hospital, the family continued to give. Over the next fifteen years, that family gave so much love and care to my parents, at a time when I lived several hours away and couldn't always meet an immediate need. They gave their time, sometimes their money, and always their heart.

And when the day came for me to clean out my parents' home, I remember being so thankful for the people that were helping me with such a difficult task. All three of those girls were there with me. Why? Because they were giving back from what they had been given, not because they felt obligated to repay a favor or a good deed, but because of what had been sown in their life many years earlier. The law of life at work. ❧

Consider this experiment with us. What would happen if it were possible to give something to every person who asked for something from us? Would it be possible to contribute—even if it was only a small amount of time or money—to every person in need who asked? We're not talking about taking on the role of "chairperson" or writing really large checks to every organization. We're simply talking about helping in some small way, doing something for everyone who asks.

What would that look like? Could we actually follow through? Well, it depends on our perspective. Because it's not the amount of the gift, it's the heart behind the gift. When Hattie gave her fifty-seven pennies, it was said that she gave more than all the other donors put together. Was hers the largest gift? No, but it came from the largest heart.

This is the "beautifully free" we would like to be.

You have not lived today until you have done something
for someone who cannot pay you back.
~ JOHN BUNYAN

The Law of Life

Whatever you give away today

or think or say or do,

will multiply about tenfold

and then return to you.

It may not come immediately

nor from the obvious source.

But the law applies unfailingly

through some invisible force.

Whatever you feel about another,

be it love or hate or passion,

will surely bounce right back to you

in some clear or secret fashion.

If you speak about some person,

a word of praise or two,

soon tens of other people will speak

kind words of you.

Giving Abundantly

Our thoughts are broadcasts of the soul,

no secrets of the brain,

kind ones bring us happiness,

petty ones untold pain.

Giving works as surely

as reflections in a mirror,

If hate you send

hate you'll get back,

but loving brings love nearer.

Remember as you start this day

and duty crowds your mind,

that kindness comes so quickly back

to those who first are kind!

Let that thought and this one

direct you through the day...

The only things we ever keep

are the things we give away![8]

CHAPTER 15

Beginning a Beautiful Journey with Purpose

PRINCIPLE 11

*E*ver watched an ant? At first glance, ants really seem to be a scattered group. They rarely walk in a straight line. They'll stop, then back up, then start again. But if you watch them long enough, you'll soon see that they always have a purposeful destination. It could be to the spilled Coke on the patio, the breadcrumbs left on the table, or back to their home.

The ants' formation is much like our life. It is a journey. Our destiny is connected to our desires. But our purpose, our reason for beginning in the first place, is the bridge that gets us there. There is a core motivation in each of us, something that causes us to do or act in every area of life. That is purpose. It's as if our willpower becomes our pull-power, pulling us toward those activities that create and accomplish our purpose.

God created you with a definite purpose in mind. Plans may change, but your purpose is constant. Your very existence is evidence that this generation needs something that your life contains. You are the creation that can produce God's desired results. But *you* are responsible for the intentional fulfillment of your purpose so the world can benefit from your contribution. In essence, you were born *for* and *with* a purpose. Your personal fulfillment is possible only to the extent that you complete your destiny.

> *To every thing there is a season,*
> *and a time to every purpose under the heaven.*
> ~ ECCLESIASTES 3:1 KJV

When you understand your purpose, you are free to live a beautiful life of abundance. You have a purpose so great that even heaven set aside a time for it to be accomplished. Your life will never have the meaning it could have unless you discover your purpose. Purpose gives you motivation and inspiration and can be the driving force that propels you to your destiny. It is one of the most important keys to a beautiful life.

Each one of us has a "beautiful" story to tell. And that story is a reflection of our purpose here on earth. You are the only one who can write the chapters in the story of your life, and the epilogue is yet to be determined. So, what will fill those pages? The experiences of your life are only part of the story. You are also creating a legacy—a piece of your life that will continue even after you are gone. Your job is to simply discover the answer to life's primary question: Why am I here? Consider this Scripture:

> *God also decided ahead of time to choose us through Christ*
> *according to his plan, which makes everything work the way*
> *he intends.* ~ Ephesians 1:11 GWT

The word "beauty" tends to connote maturity, fulfillment, and a perfecting of the qualities that were designed specifically for you. What you need to know is that everything has been created with a purpose.

And every purpose requires time to turn a simple life into a beautiful life, and then to take a beautiful life and make it perfect. So, know this: God makes everything beautiful in its time.

Think about a rose. During the winter it lies dormant, a time that is necessary for it to grow into the beautiful flower it was created to become—a fragrant and a beautiful rose, enjoyed by everyone who sees it. In the spring, a rose is not all that attractive. Thorns cover the stems and tiny, hard, green things stick out among the leaves. But slowly, those green things begin to open, and individual petals begin to come to the surface. Even then, it's not complete. Eventually, however, the rose reaches its ultimate beauty. Through patience and perseverance, the rose writes its story. Are you writing yours?

Tomorrow

She was going to be all she wanted to be—tomorrow.

None would be kinder or braver than she—tomorrow.

A friend who was troubled and weary, she knew,

Who would be glad of a life like hers, and needed it too.

On her way, she would call and see what she could do—tomorrow.

Each morning she would stack up the letters she's written—tomorrow

And thought of the folks she could fill with delight—tomorrow.

And hadn't one moment to stop on her way.

For "more time I will give others," she'd say—tomorrow.

The greatest of workers this girl would have been—tomorrow.

The world would have hailed her if she'd ever been—tomorrow.

But in fact she passed on and faded from view,

and all that was left here when living was through,

was a mountain of things she intended to do—tomorrow.

Many people go to their grave never living out their purpose. But some people refuse to let their stories be buried with them. Consider the following:

She was born in a small town in Mississippi in 1954. Her father was in the service and her mother moved to Milwaukee, Wisconsin, in search of a new start, leaving her behind. She was raised by her paternal grandmother on a small farm. Her grandmother taught her to read before most children were ready for pre-school. And because of her grandmother's strong Christian background, she was very active in the church. By the time she was three, she had traveled through the South reciting sermons and Bible verses.

By the age of six, she moved into her mother's home, which was a far cry from the supportive, safe environment she had been used to. Her childhood took a drastic turn when she was forced to endure repeated sexual abuse. Reading was her only escape.

By the age of fourteen, she was pregnant by one of her abusers. The baby was premature and died shortly after it was born. Her mother couldn't handle her puberty and declared her "incorrigible," sending her to live with her father.

Her new home in Tennessee was nothing like the wild, "party house" atmosphere of her mother's home. Her father demanded good study habits and high morals. He was a strict disciplinarian and helped her to adopt a new standard of living.

In high school, she began to refine her natural public speaking talent by participating in the production of a regular radio show. She was also encouraged to compete in pageants where she awed the judges and mesmerized the crowd with her public speaking. Her father was supportive of her success. Under his guidance, she landed a full scholarship to Tennessee State University.

She knew she was in a unique position. In 1971 not many impoverished, abused black girls were given the opportunity to attend any university. Her father had instilled in her a powerful work ethic, which complemented the high moral beliefs of her grandmother.

By the time she was in her sophomore year of college, her career was well on its way, as she had become the youngest person, the first African-American, and the first woman to anchor a newscast in Nashville at WTVF-TV. In 1976, she moved to Baltimore where she worked as a reporter and co-anchor for WJZ-TV. A year later, she won the coveted position of co-host on the major morning news/talk show "People Are Talking." Eight years in Baltimore led to an invitation to move to Illinois and host "AM Chicago." She accepted the opportunity and was pitted against Phil Donohue, who had been number one in that time slot for quite a while. She, however, beat him in the ratings. And her talk show remained the highest rated talk show in the years that followed.

Producers recognized her power and appeal immediately. The following year, her talk show was syndicated and she began her film career. A smart businesswoman, Oprah Winfrey soon owned HARPO Productions, HARPO Films, HARPO Studios, and HARPO Video. Not content just to star in a Spielberg film, she monopolized the technical production as well!

Her conversational interview style and friendly, empathetic nature have been major factors in her success. For many women, an hour watching "The Oprah Winfrey Show" is as refreshing as an hour spent sipping coffee with a friend. Her personal tragedies and successes have motivated her and driven her to success. She speaks openly and freely of the events in her life and challenges many women to better themselves.

At the dawn of the new millennium, Oprah became one of the partners in Oxygen Media, Inc., a cable channel and interactive network for women, followed by *O, The Oprah Magazine.* Now a media giant, she has unprecedented presence in the homes of her viewers. Her self-improvement success has been the inspiration for much of her recent success. She urges viewers to better themselves through education, service to others, and responsible consumerism.

And she is a giver. In 1997, she began the Oprah's Angel Network as a fundraiser to help those in need. Her efforts have built over two hundred Habitat-for-Humanity homes and sent hundreds of disadvantaged youth to college. Her empire grows every year.[19] And she has proven that she was not afraid to write her "beautiful" story.

Your story is no less powerful. Looking at Oprah's life, you may think there's no way you can ever accomplish what she has. You may even say to yourself, *Why bother?* But you have to bother because there's no telling who needs that one thing that only you can offer.

It's up to you to create your own story, your own beautiful life. And, if you don't create that story, you'll always regret it. You may experience more stress, which often leads to burnout. You may have difficulty making decisions, which often leads to taking on more than you can handle. You could spend your life comparing yourself to others, which can lead to resentment. You may find yourself living with past mistakes, which takes away the joy of today.

If you refuse to write your story, your life won't be filled with joy or bring happiness and fulfillment. You'll find yourself focusing far more on your weaknesses than on your strengths. In essence, life without purpose is really no life at all.

"But I don't have a burning desire to pursue anything in particular," you may be saying. "I know I could be good at something, but I sure don't know what that something is." Some of you still aren't sure what you want to be when you grow up—and you've been grown up for quite some time now. Is this where you are? If so, it's time to dig down to the very core of your being. Think about the instincts you've been given. Your instincts are signals from God, the inner voice that you sense within you. Listen to those feelings. Pray over them. Then, take the steps necessary to follow them through. If you allow them to surface, they will steer you toward the true passions of your life. Passion is the very fuel for dreams. And if you'll listen, you'll begin to wake up each morning living to work, rather than working to live.

We challenge you to spend the next few weeks journaling every day. Use that time to express yourself through a detailed examination of your life. As you begin to uncover the gifts and passions God has given you, what you will discover will be a purposeful, beautiful life.

As you journal, here are some of the questions you can ask yourself to begin your story:

- What kind of experiences or activities do I look forward to?
- What excites me?
- What would get me out of bed early and make me stay up late? (It could be anything from sports, to shopping, to listening to great music, to journaling, to spending time with those who are important to you.)
- What are my skills and talents?
- What do I like to do that might seem totally mundane to someone else? (Try to list at least five to ten activities that you truly love.)
- What skills do I have that seem to align with the things I'm most passionate about?

When you've answered these questions, you might find that your answers are surprising. But if you take the time to truly open your eyes to your passions, you may discover they are the very "bridges" that will take you to your destiny.

Now get out there! Go do it! Begin to discover your purpose! And when you do, you've just discovered the bridge to becoming, free, *free to be beautiful.*

PART III

For an Extraordinary Life

CHAPTER 16

Free to Be Beautiful

*O*kay stand up. Yes really! Read the following out loud. Yes really!

I will let no one push my buttons.
I will let no one rain on my parade.
I will go over, I will go under,
I will go around and I will go through
any obstacle that comes my way!
I will not hesitate in the presence of procrastination,
negotiate at the table of fear,
ponder at the pool of popularity,
or meander in the maze of mediocrity.
I won't give up, shut up, let up,
until I've stayed up, stored up, prayed up, and paid up,
and become the person that God intended me to be.
What I think about, I bring about,
look out and have no doubt,
when I am committed that's when I stand out.
By affirming I am instantly inspired, highly motivated,
truly dedicated to becoming the woman I will be!

How's that? That is an affirmation. Say it, seize it, claim it!

We've come a long way, haven't we? We've dealt with our attitude and our relationships. We've learned the value of seizing today and letting go of our past. We've laid out personal plans of growth and realized that change is possible and choices matter. We've learned the power of giving and the power of gratitude. We've learned that our purpose is key to each one of these things. But each step, when combined with the others, culminates in the joy of being *free to be beautiful.* And the thread that's woven through each step in the journey is faith.

Faith is essential if we want to be successful in our attitude, our growth, our purpose, and most of all, our freedom. Without faith, we'll never discover any of these. We all have faith in something. But not all of us choose to use it to promote beautiful outcomes. Some of us say, "Nothing good ever happens to me." Or, "If it weren't for bad luck, I wouldn't have any luck at all." Or, "These kinds of things just always seem to happen to me." Or, "Nothing ever works out for me." These are all statements of faith. Those speaking these statements have total confidence that what they are saying is true. Even more terrifying is the fact they believe there is nothing they can do to change it. So they get what they expect, because expectations are fueled by faith.

But *you* can have faith of another kind:

> Faith that can make you an adventurer. You can let go of the past and conquer your fears.
> Faith that can expose your true values and give you new ones to strive for.
> Faith that can allow you to examine your perspectives and attitudes.
> Faith that you can have a grateful heart.
> Faith that can show you love and then teach you how to love others.

Faith that today is a gift, and that you can seize it and
make the most of it.
Faith that can guide you to make beautiful changes.
Faith that can strengthen you to make beautiful choices.
Faith that can propel you to plan your life and discover
your future.
Faith that you can give generously.
Faith that your purpose can be revealed and that you can
begin to live "on purpose."
Faith that you can learn to expect the impossible and
then make it happen.
Faith that *you can believe* in *you*.

So may we encourage you once again?

Never stop learning. No matter how old you get and how much
you learn, you can never know it all. There's always someone wiser
who can teach you something you never knew. There's always a book
with information you've never thought of. There's always an experience
yet to be discovered. Take advantage of every resource to learn more.
Learning will allow you to go places you never would have been able
to travel.

Be persistent. Life is a marathon, not a sprint. Don't look for the
short-term gain, but keep your heart focused on longterm discoveries.
Be persistent in affirming that you are capable of doing everything necessary to accomplish your dreams. If you have to write it down, get out
that pen. If you need to visualize it, paint yourself a picture. And if you
need to say it out loud, buy yourself a megaphone. But don't let
anything cause you to run out of steam.

Learn to do and enjoy the little things. Don't make life all about the
"big" task. Make it about doing the small things well. And eventually, by
being diligent in the small things, you will have accomplished the great.

Deal and communicate with people effectively. People are a part
of the experience. Some will aggravate you; others will crack you up.
Love them both. Affirm them both. Smile at them both. And don't let
anything separate you from your goal of enjoying a beautiful life with
those that you walk with from beginning to end.

Be honest and be dependable. The world offers a thousand
journeymen. But few can be characterized by their integrity. Choose to
be one that is. Take responsibility for yourself and make your contribution to this world. It will appreciate you for what you've given.

The future belongs to those who believe in the beauty of their dreams.
- ELEANOR ROOSEVELT

It's not the size of your dreams that matters; it's the fact that you
have a dream in the first place. You *can* create the life of your dreams!
We're living proof. And we are here to remind you that there is nothing in this world that you can't accomplish. You are never too young or
too old. It doesn't matter how swamped you may feel today or if fear
has left you quaking in your Anne Klein, knee-high boots.

Dreams don't arrive on the doorstep of those smart enough to have
one. They arrive on the doorstep of those smart enough to open the
door. They aren't relegated by your height or your birthright. They
aren't a by-product of good skin or good luck. No, the key to having
what you want is knowing what you want!

Do you? Are you living life at the mercy of others, or for the call of
your own heart? If you went into a restaurant knowing that you would
have to eat whatever the waiter chose for you, would you really want to
go? What if it were sushi or liver? Would you want to only wear the
clothes someone else picked out for you, even if that person didn't
know you or maybe even like you? You could end up in a muumuu or
a tube top.

You wouldn't live any other part of your day based on other people's desires for your life. So, don't let your dreams fall to anyone else either. You know what you want. You have expectations in your heart. So it's up to you to determine what the outcome will be. Take charge of your dreams.

God uses what you have to fill a need you never could have filled.
God uses where you are to take you where you never could have gone.
God uses what you can do to accomplish what you never could have done.
God uses who you are to let you become who you never could have been.
- PHILIP CLARKE BREWER

We could offer you a thousand options for living life. We could wrap them in different packages and paint them in colors that you could enjoy. But our greatest desire is that you discover the gift of you and discover the gift of being free, *free to be beautiful.*

But to as many as did receive and welcomed Him, He gave the authority
(power, privilege, right) to become the children [daughter] of God, that is,
to those who believe in (adhere to, trust in, and rely on) His name.
- JOHN 1:12 AMPLIFIED

Would you go one step farther with us? There's nothing we enjoy more than having lunch together. Would you please join us for an imaginary lunch? You pick the place. We love it all: burgers, chicken, steak, even Chinese. We guarantee that whatever is on the menu at your favorite place, we'll enjoy it.

We'll talk about our spouses, or the one you're hoping to find. We'll spend some time catching up on the kids, their first kisses, their latest achievements, their impending arrivals, or the yet-met treasure of what they might be. We'll talk about the weight we've lost or the weight we've gained. And then we'll be thankful for the Diet Coke that comes with our meal.

We'll talk about what we've discovered about ourselves along this journey we've taken together—the attitudes we've had to adjust, the past we've had to release, the purpose we've discovered that was there all along. And then, we'll give you a gift.

You'll act shocked, sincerely or not, but you'll want to make us feel good, so you'll look surprised. And you'll open it, having no idea what it is. At least, we hope you won't or it might ruin the surprise. Under the pink tissue paper (we love pink!), you'll catch a glimpse of something shiny. As you pull out the crown, you'll smile because now you know. You might not have realized it a couple of months ago when we started this journey, but it's crystal clear now. You are a princess.

And you know what else this crown will remind you of? All the wonders of life and living that you are entitled to. Entitled to enjoy today and everything it has to offer. Entitled to love with abandon those things you once found unlovely. Entitled to give of yourself, of your abilities, of your wisdom. And entitled to dream—something that you might have even forgotten to do until now. But not today. Today, your dreams are bombarding you. In fact, you're wondering if you'll even be able to keep up! You will. You'll surprise yourself. Your dreams will grow you, and as they do, you will have discovered that the principles of commoners have created royalty. That the ordinary principles of living have produced an extraordinary life.

And then when we get up to leave, we'll pay the check. Oh, don't even fight us over it. Today is about *you*. We'll hug each other and tell each other that we need to do this again very soon. We'll try not to cry, but we won't try too hard because, after all, that's what women do.

We'll watch as you walk to your car, and we'll be so proud of you. And then we'll remind ourselves of all the things we've learned together. And we'll be thankful that we took this journey to freedom together.

That you may really come to know, experience for yourselves, the love of Christ, which far surpasses mere knowledge. That you may be filled through all your being, with the richest measure of the divine presence of God. And believe you are the beautiful daughter that He declares you to be.

You are, you know. You're free, *free to be beautiful.*

❧

A Beautiful Prayer

*T*hank you, Lord, that You are good!

Your faithful love endures forever.

You have loved me with an everlasting love and with unfailing love

You have drawn me to You.

As I receive your love and forgiveness, I am able to let go of the past.

I give my fears to you and trust that

You are able to carry what I've placed in your care.

Yesterday is gone, and I am thankful for the gift of today.

I look in the mirror of Your Word to reflect on and establish my

values as they lay the groundwork for my success in life.

Thank you, Lord, for an attitude to do all things without complaining,

fault-finding, and arguing in order that I may live free to be beautiful.

Help me to choose to maintain a sincere attitude of gratitude,

having motives that honor You.

I want to be a woman who accepts gratefully, with a thankful

heart, the life that you have given me.

I deeply desire to develop and nurture my relationship with You and

choose to "seize the day" by starting each one becoming Your friend.

With every person I know, help me to live to forgive, just as You forgive me.

I'll live doing for them as I would have them do for me.

Create in me a desire to grow and develop personally everyday,

Planning to become more.

With your help, I will make positive choices that will grow a fruitful, confident, and beautiful life.

I choose to think about and put into practice the necessary steps that will produce the change that helps me grow.

I will practice and cultivate a generous, giving heart.

I give abundantly and wholeheartedly knowing it's impossible to outgive You.

With perfect timing, you fashioned me with purpose!

Help me, Lord, to stay motivated and inspired, living to maximize the potential for which I was created, in order to tell the beautiful story of the life you so graciously have given me.

Help me to dream and live with courageous faith, believing that I am Free... Free to be Beautiful.

FREE TO BE BEAUTIFUL PERMISSION SLIP

Today is a defining moment.

I choose to believe that God has a purpose for my life.

When God fashioned me, He placed inside my heart the dream to live a free and beautiful life.

I accept the plan He has for me and receive that He is enthralled with my beauty.

With a grateful heart, I thank Him for the opportunity to make choices, plan my personal growth, and make the necessary changes in order to live giving and serving others.

Inspired by faith, I agree to let go of the past, reflect on and define my values, and take responsibility for a positive attitude.

I commit to rereading the beautiful principles in this book often and applying them in order to live the beautiful life that is available to me.

Today, I give myself permission to begin and become *free to be beautiful* and will read this commitment often.

Name: ———————————————————— Date: —————————

It's a Beautiful Sisterhood!

OUR JOURNEY TOGETHER DOESN'T HAVE TO STOP AT THE END OF THIS BOOK.

We are never too young, too old or too busy to take a step and journey toward a free and beautiful life. We want you to join us.

We've mentored hundreds of our girlfriends in the last few years and this sisterhood is calling your name to be included!

Receive a **FREE** Mentoring Resource Today!

Visit **www.FreetoBeBeautiful.com** to find out about how to receive tools and resources designed to keep you believing and becoming free to be beautiful.

YOUR DREAMS ARE WORTH IT!

Read inspiring stories of girlfriends practicing the *"Free to Be Beautiful"* principles. Beautiful and unstoppable women who continue the process of transformation each day.

We care about your progress, and we want to hear your story. Would you share with us the ups and downs and in-betweens of your discoveries?

If you will, we will send you a *Free and Beautiful* mentoring resource that is sure to encourage you. Our gift to you for sharing with us. So don't wait...

Sign-up at **www.FreetoBeBeautiful.com** Today!

DIVINE INTERVENTION: HOW WE MET

Tina remembers:

Nearly four years ago, I received a call to sing a song on a particular new music project. Nothing new there.

Six months later, I was asked to come back and record six more songs for this same project. While I was in the studio, Karen Ford, the woman who commissioned the project called. She had heard some of the initial songs and was impressed. "Would you be willing to sing these songs for an event in Gatlinburg I'm having?" she asked.

"I know it's last minute, and I've spent all my budget, but I can certainly pay your travel expenses." Now *this* was new. Karen urged me to consider coming to entertain and inspire the four hundred women who would be attending the event. This, I came to realize later, is one of Karen's gifts: gentle "urging."

Come for nothing? I thought. I had never met Karen Ford. I didn't even know what she looked like, and I wasn't sure I wanted to give up a full weekend to sing for her. Besides, it was a step out of my comfort zone since I had been spending most of my "singing" time as a studio singer and worship leader in churches.

I told her I needed to check my schedule and would call her back. This gave me a chance to consider it before I just said, "Thank you very much but ... no!"

My husband and I discussed this "opportunity" to travel four hours and entertain women for free. While a big part of me just dreaded the thought of doing this, deep down inside I really felt that it was something I should do. I called Karen the next day and said that I would come.

Two days later, Karen called again. "Tina, I forgot to tell you, the theme for our event is centered around Cinderella and the stage will be complete with castle and carriage. We have a Cinderella gown that we'd like you to wear. You'll sing the last song in the gown, complete with silver-glitter shoes, tiara, and scepter. You will walk around their tables singing to them. It will be great!"

I nearly dropped the phone! What had I gotten myself into? A Cinderella gown? This is not what I do! I've never considered myself an entertainer, and I'm certainly not a princess. Karen couldn't be serious, could she? She was. This was beyond gently urging. She actually thought it was a good idea for me to dress up like Cinderella and prance around the stage!

I met Karen for the first time at sound check, thirty minutes before the event started, and I immediately connected with her. I liked her and knew it was going to be a fun weekend. I decided to go ahead and play "Cinderella"—and believe it or not, I had a great time!

A few days after returning to Nashville, Karen and I had lunch together. And then we had more. We both sensed there was more to our meeting and decided to spend time together in order to consider what it was. As it turns out, there was. We learned that we shared many of the same dreams. Writing this book was one of them.

Karen, thanks for sharing this dream with me. Writing *Free To Be Beautiful* has been a most amazing experience. Your extraordinary life is one to follow and I'm glad to have the opportunity to do so. Thanks, girlfriend.

~ PRINCESS TINA

Karen remembers:

Four years ago, it was a particularly busy day in my office as we were working on final preparations for our *big* annual event that was just days away. Most all of the plans had been made and the budget was exhausted.

Jason, a friend of a friend, had been working on a music project for the event, and in the early afternoon, he dropped the final copy of the CD off for me to hear. I knew that CD was going to make a difference for our consultants that year, so I stopped what I was doing and excitedly put the CD in the player. With each song, I was more and more elated, and was especially impressed with the female vocalist—someone I didn't even know was going to be on the CD. I felt I could actually "hear" her smile between the notes of the music. I definitely heard her heart.

I picked up the phone and called Jason and told him how impressed I was with the project and especially the songs that featured that beautiful, smiling voice. He explained that she was a friend of his. I asked for her name and number because when the event was over, I wanted to call and thank her for her part in the project. This was a little odd in itself since it is generally my practice to simply write a thank you note, rather than make a thank you call.

Without really knowing why, I immediately dialed Tina's number and she answered the phone. In a world where we generally leave a voicemail so that we can get a voicemail in return, this again was a little unusual. My intent was to simply say "thank you" instead, I found myself asking Tina if she would consider attending our event and performing the music live. I confessed that there was really no money in the budget to pay her, but I would cover her expenses if she would consider it. As I spoke the words I was thinking to myself, *How absurd—to ask someone I have never met to do something for me without any expectation of payment for the services!* And besides, I had already contracted a person to sing and perform. I would never cancel at the last minute on that willing person!

Tina immediately responded that she would consider it and get back to me the next day. I hung up the phone never expecting that she would agree, but knowing that I really wanted my people to experience her music live. I figured that I knew what her answer was going to be, so I got back to work tying up loose ends for the event and didn't give it much thought the rest of that busy day.

The next morning—true to her word—Tina called to give me her answer. I expected that it would be a short conversation and that she would be polite as she expressed regret that she could not make it this time.

Surprise! Tina agreed to attend. My mind began racing: *What am I going to do now to handle two performers gracefully?* Then I had an idea. Just so you know, my assistant hates to hear those words right before an event; she would rather hear anything other than "I have an idea"!

I immediately thanked Tina and began to tell her of my idea—that she had no idea had just popped into my head. The theme for that year was "Making Dreams Happen," and I was using some of the fairy tale ideas to make it fun. I told Tina that I would like to have her dressed as Cinderella at the closing dinner, and sing a special song as she made her entrance through the crowd to come to the stage. I assured her that I would take care of the rental fees for the Cinderella gown complete with tiara, scepter, and maybe even some real glass slippers. There was silence on the other end of the phone, and I was sure that I had probably gone too far, asking such a thing from a person I had never even met. It was so out of character for me to plan such a major thing on the spur of the moment—with none of it in the budget. There was nothing left in the budget!

Then Tina spoke: "Well, Karen, I guess I could do that, but you really need to know I am *not* the Cinderella type. I am short, I am not the Cinderella size, and I have never really done anything like that." I said, "Great! Give my assistant your size, and we'll make sure that we have everything you need to be Cinderella at our awards banquet!" I thanked her again and told her I would see her in Gatlinburg the next week!

I then began trying to figure out how I was going to plan the agenda to accommodate *two* performers and give them both the time they deserved. Well, I figured, we'll just have to have a lot of music at this particular event.

Very late the evening before the event was to begin, I arrived at the hotel in Gatlinburg and received the message that Tina and her husband were there and would be down early for a sound check the next morning. I planned to be there for the sound check, so that I could finally meet my new friend for the very first time.

We spoke briefly before the event began. I thanked her for coming and gave her an agenda. I told her we would get a chance to talk after the awards banquet the next night.

The event was a great success! Yes, we had a lot of music that weekend, and I had to cut some other things so that both performers could shine. But I didn't care because I knew that everyone there could hear the smile in Tina's voice and the heart in the song when she performed. And. . . that evening, at the awards banquet, "Cinderella" did a fabulous job, entering the room from the back, walking through the audience, and singing to them as she made her way to the stage.

Afterward, there was about an hour of Kodak moments for each one that wanted to have her picture made with the real, live "Cinderella." It was the perfect ending to a wonderful weekend, and I knew that those women were inspired to pursue their own dreams in the weeks to come.

After that event, Tina and I agreed to have lunch and get to know each other a bit. We met for lunch a few weeks later and had a very long, wonderful afternoon getting to know each other. We didn't really finish everything we had to say, so we agreed to meet again. And so began a wonderful friendship and a connection that I really didn't understand.

It was about the fourth lunch that we looked at each other and expressed that we really didn't know why we kept meeting for lunch, but that for some reason we both knew it was the right thing to do. Even though neither of us really had the time in our schedules to justify these lunches on such a regular basis, we knew we needed to keep meeting.

In our hearts, we both knew that if we kept "meeting and eating," when the time was right God would let us in on His plan. Until then, we would just enjoy lunch!

~ KAREN

NOTES

1. Princess Diana Biographical information: Newsweek, Commemorative Issue, "Diana: A Celebration of her life," November 3, 1997; *People*, "Goodbye, Diana," September 22, 1997; *People*, September 15, 1997.

2. Mother Theresa Biographical information: *No Greater Love* (MJF Books, 1997), 101.

3. http://www.strategiccoach.com/ideas/artcl_uniqueAbility.shtml, (last accessed 3.17.2005).

4. Adapted from "The Guy in the Glass" by Peter Wimbrow Sr., copyright 1934, *American*.

5. Dave Ramsey, *How to Have More than Enough, A Step-by-Step Guide to Creating Abundance* (New York: Penguin Books, 2000), 22.

6. John C. Maxwell, *The Winning Attitude: Your Key to Personal Success* (Nashville: Thomas Nelson, 1993, 24.

7. Matthew 25:14-30.

8. Adapted from "Do it Anyway," by Mother Teresa as found in *Simple Path* (New York: Ballantine Books, 1995), 185.

9. Luke 17:11-19.

10. "Serenity Prayer:" http://www.aahistory.com/prayer.html, (last accessed 3.17.2005).

11. "An Irish Prayer:" http://www.gallagher.com/prayer.htm, (last accessed 3.17.2005).

12. "Through Me," by Roy Lessin, DaySpring Cards. (This poem came from a plaque that hangs on Karen's wall.)

13. "You Can Have It All" 1997 Calendar, Lifetime Wisdom from America's Foremost Woman Entrepreneur, Andrews and McMeel, A Universal Press Syndicate Company-Kansas City, copyright 1996, Mary Kay, Inc. printed in the USA. January 20, 1997 and January 21, 1997.

14. "Tomorrow", by Charles Strouse & Martin Charnin Copyright 1977, Edwin H. Morris & Company, A Division of MPL Communications, Inc. and Charles Strouse, From the Musical "Annie," Published 1977.

15. John C. Maxwell, "How to Make Personal Changes in Your Life," *Maximum Impact*, Volume 6, Number 10.

16. "Power of Choice" by Fr. Norbert Weber: www.appleseeds.org/power_of.htm, (last accessed 3.17.2005).

17. "Story of Hattie" as found in *From My Heart to Yours*, 1990.

18. Jerry Buchanan, "The Law of Life," *From My Heart to Yours*, 1990.

19. Oprah Winfrey Biographical information: http://inin.essortment.com/oprahwinfreybi_rmjm.htm, (last accessed 3.17.2005).